EARTH BOY

BILLY THOMPSON

To Joe R who loved all creatures and wanted to change the world who also once said: One day, Earth Boy, tell your story.

To Jill Phipps who we will never forget for her courage, commitment and the ultimate sacrifice of her life for the animals. Diamond the Shetland pony. An early blossom taken by an unexpected frost. And a pig called Zachariah.

— Rita —

EARTH BOY

A million thanks for
your kindness to the foxes
with gratitude
Billy xxp

Earth Boy

Published by The Conrad Press Ltd. in the United Kingdom 2021

Tel: +44(0)1227 472 874
www.theconradpress.com
info@theconradpress.com

ISBN 978-1-914913-27-3

Printed and bound in Great Britain by Clays Ltd, Elcograf S.p.A

Cover illustration by Abbie Sibun

Typesetting and Cover Design by The Book Typesetters
www.thebooktypesetters.com

The Conrad Press logo was designed by Maria Priestley.

CONTENTS

CONTENTS

PREFACE

This is no usual animal rescue story of chocolate box puppies and kittens. It's a tale of how wherever you are and whatever you are doing you can always show compassion and help animals. From picking up injured pigeons from busy streets to neutering colonies of feral cats. From converting a garden shed to offer respite to a needy animal to renting a field to save farm animals from slaughter. From negotiating the freedom of failed racehorses so not to end up on someone's plate, to bringing home stray street dogs from abroad. There's something everyone can do. We are all ordinary people but let's try and do something extraordinary.

Be kind, it's easy.

Billy H Thompson
Founder & Project Director
The Retreat Animal Rescue & Café
Brickyard Farm
Cripple Hill
High Halden
Kent TN26 3 LJ

07720495238
www.retreatanimalrescue.org.uk
Charity number 1105654

CHAPTER ONE

FAMILY

There's no better place to start this tour of my life than at the beginning. For each stage shows a stepping stone, however subtle of the shape of things to come. It shows that unique friendship with all beings is only a blink of an eye away from something very remarkable. There's no need to look out for them. You're like a magnet; they will find you. Just stay happy, keep that smile on your face and radiate positivity it's the key to living the life you want.

And so my story begins: I arrived in the delivery ward of the world-famous Guy's Hospital London at approximately 1:30pm on 11th May 1968. With my mum in labour my dad drove her to the hospital and dropped the expecting mother off all by herself (apparently in those days dads didn't stay). Both my parents are dedicated family people, hard-working and generous to a fault, if not a little crazy too. Both love their children and have always wanted the best for them. We have remained a happy family unit who live close by each other. We still enjoy the company of each other on holidays together and try our best to have Sunday dinner together during the winter. Our lives remain interwoven and have created the colourful tapestry we live in today. They are the type of people who will help anyone, always there with a helping hand and a listening ear.

My parents met when they were both in their twenties when my mum was a real dolly bird who boasted long bouncing blonde hair, false eyelashes, five-inch heels and a mini skirt. She worked as a barmaid in the Thomas A Becket pub on the Old Kent Road London and my dad was a tall handsome bachelor who walked in all suntanned from a trip to Mallorca, his blue Ford Zephyr parked outside to let the girls know he had arrived. Back then my dad was known as 'Flash Harry'; he would show off his rolls of bank notes, never letting on they were packed out with toilet paper. The first meeting led to another and soon they were courting. It didn't take long for him to pop the question and my delighted mum said yes. Almost two years later they were married at St Crispin and Christ Church, Southwark Park Road, Bermondsey. A celebrated union with all the family there to witness the happy couple say 'I do'.

Thankfully I was an easy birth. My mum had gone into labour that morning whilst cooking breakfast for my dad and then carried on with the house chores until my dad would drive her to the hospital. Born with a healthy-looking colour because I was jaundice and nicknamed 'Mr Universe' by the nurses, I took to life with a smile on my face. A proud moment for my dad even if it was during the Saturday afternoon races and on receiving the call from my mum that everything went well and 'it's a boy', he went straight to the pub with his dad to celebrate and not to the hospital to see me or my mum.

Maybe he had an idea of the things to come with me and that only a stiff drink could sort out. I had two sets of thrilled grandparents because I was the first grandson. The next ten days my mum and I spent our time in the hospital with a visit each day from my dad and grandparents. As the gifts of soft toy animals arrived, little did they know that the tiny newborn would have such a passion for helping all creatures great and small.

Animals have been my life force since I can remember. They run through my veins and straight into my heart. If they hurt, I hurt, and I'll do absolutely anything to stop them hurting. They have shared every step of my journey and supported me through the ups and downs life serves us all. From the death of a loved one to heartbreak and even tears of happiness, they show their unconditional love each and every time with a paw, a lick, a bark or just laying next to you when you most needed a friend.

I've shared my whole life with animals. My earliest memories are those with all sorts of creatures and making sure they had everything they needed and more. I can never remember a time without fur, fin or feather. At the age of only two my maternal grandmother, Nanny Glad, allowed me a small, fenced space in her London garden to keep cats, ducks and rabbits. Here I would sit and tend my latest baby for hours. Although I was very young for such responsibilities, I had the wonderful guidance of many animal lovers in my family. These tiny baby animals and birds I loved and kept safe were acquired at local pet markets like Club Row – places that I would one day work to close down as an animal rights activist and campaigner.

Three years later my mum and dad gave birth to my partner in crime in animal rescue: my little sister Lil. Thankfully growing up with a sibling that cares equally about animals has made my life much easier by sharing ideas to help the plight of animals and establishing many rescue projects. Lil, unlike me, had a business head just like Mum and Dad, whilst I was the dreamer. With the three of them behind me anything was possible.

One of my first animal friendships that I remember well was a beautifully loyal Labrador called Adam who was fiercely protective of us all. He had been in our family from only six weeks old. At the time of his arrival we lived in rented rooms and then quickly moved on to above our pub, The Clarence, on the Jamaica Road. My mum, being one of the hardest-working parents I've ever met and an impulsive entrepreneur, came home from 'popping out to get some potatoes' returned with smiles to tell my dad she was now taking over the lease of the greengrocers and flower shop.

One night when my parents went out and left us with a new babysitter, Adam, our family dog, famously tore her fur coat to pieces because she went near our bedrooms to check up on us. Terrified not to move she waited by the stairs until my parents returned, watching Adam tearing every last part of the new coat into bite-size pieces. Looking back, he must have been an advocate for a fur-free London and knew just how cruel real fur is. Another act of Adam's protectiveness was when my sister and I climbed a tree in our local park but couldn't get down, and he wouldn't let anyone help us. Adam sat at the bottom of the tree growling at anyone coming to our calls of help. Thankfully, a kind neighbour alerted my mum and down to the park she came to free us from the tree. Adam was our protector and would always be praised for keeping us safe however inconvenient his antics were.

Another great dog friend of mine was my headmistress Mrs Lloyd's apricot toy poodle, called Tigger, who I adored and often carried to the sandpit to help me dig and build castles. These dogs are not only in my memory but my heart too. These early creatures are instrumental in showing me just how unique all creatures are and that they're happy to be part of a human family, if loved. I can only ever remember loving and caring for the natural world. Fascinated with everything nature had to offer from trees I could climb, colourful spring bulbs, assorted fruits growing on trees, the constellations and the different moons but most of all the creatures of planet earth. I grew up in South East London where everyone knew everyone. A community of people who would do anything for anyone. Doors never locked and neighbours popped in and a pot of tea was everyone's problem solver. 'Stick the kettle on' was a normal term of endearment.

Everyone had an animal. My Aunty Bet and Uncle Len had a big yellow budgie called Billy. Billy lived a long and healthy life of eighteen years and would pick at Uncle Len's teeth and drink from his glass, and was a great companion to Bet and Len. Our neighbours, Eileen and Terry, had a three-legged tabby cat called Henry, who turned out to be Henrietta when she had her kittens behind their stove. Animals were everywhere and remain in every memory.

Our flower shop was situated in the heart of our community on Jamaica Road, which ran from the Rotherhithe Tunnel at one end, into Tooley Street at the other, meeting the iconic Tower Bridge. The shop, situated in a small modern parade under a block of flats, was only fifty meters from the park gates. Southwark Park had large open fields, long grasses, mature London plane trees to climb and a beautiful pond and rose garden where feeding the birds and ducks was a daily must on the way home from school.

Each season in the park taught me something different. Autumn with piles of leaves to play in and run through also showed me it was home to insects nesting down deep inside for the warmth. The duck pond freezing over in winter had me wondering if the ducks got frozen or cold legs. I enjoyed the many different shapes and sizes of spring flowers and the summer's abundance of goodwill to London's wildlife. I loved watching birds building their nests and feeding pigeons who would land on my hands held out to feast on freshly cracked peanuts. Then there was the grey squirrel happily making friends with anyone who had a carrier bag of food – such an easy friendship to be made. I adored the squirrels, liking them to large wild hamsters and I can remember looking for the same one everyday who had a toe missing. These wild creatures I thought of as my friends and remember packing the carrier bag with nuts, bread and peelings and thinking who would most enjoy the different treats. I would return home with pockets filled with leaves, stones, twigs and sycamore seeds we called helicopters. I would throw the seeds up and watch them helicopter down around me, a treat only in the darker months.

London was a safe and exciting place to live for any child. Surprisingly, it had many open spaces and of course the great River Thames. You were never short of something to do or somewhere to explore. Animals knew they could trust me, and I would keep them safe. I would move snails from the hazards of busy paths, pick up injured butterflies and put them on the nearest blossoms, rescue stranded beetles in containers full of rainwater, even save trapped flies from spider webs. Every day was an opportunity to help some creature somewhere.

I was born a rescuer. Early memories of rescues included the time walking home from school with my mum and sister when we saw Lucky, the local latch-key dog, chasing a rather fat cat. The cat ran under the workman's hut and when my mum saw off Lucky the dog with a loud shout of 'leave her alone!', we realised the cat was not fat but a poor pregnant stray. My mum showed me how I could slide under the shed and bring out the scared feline. I crawled around in the dark until I could find the crying moggy, I grabbed her tight. I emerged triumphantly from under the building with a beautiful tabby mum-to-be in my arms.

So pleased to have her safe, we set off home and I thought to myself how I loved her soft fur and wide eyes and prayed we could keep her. Once we got her home and explained how much she needed us it didn't take much to persuade my dad she needed a safe place to have her babies. We made her a comfy bed in a flower box and fed her enough food to feed an army. We called her Mitzi and within days she produced four amazing little bundles of joy. The first two were huge, a black fluffy female called Clio and a big tabby boy called Cassius. The next two were tiny and we called them Lucky and Mistral. They were so cold and weak, unable to feed, so we hand-reared them alongside Mum until they were four weeks old and started eating solids with their siblings.

There are times when my mum is at her wit's end with me, asking where I got this obsession from, with my endless escapades to save animals. I would remind her of how she trained me at only eight in pure superhero style to slide under a building and rescue such a poor creature. 'Trained by the best', I now remind her. This rescue of Mum and kittens is one of my happiest memories and one of my proudest moments. I was only eight years old and already rescuing the neediest of street strays.

My favourite toy was always my plastic farm set which contained tractor, farmhouse and barns, all farm animals with their young, a farmer, his wife, and a dog. For a birthday present I also received an animal transporter and new packs of farm animals. Where for most children the transporter would fill up with the farm animals and drive them away, my transporter, even if I didn't know it then, was a rescue lorry driving off and filling up with animals to return to the safety of my plastic rescue centre. When asked by my dad why I didn't get rid of some of the animals I replied that this was their home, and here they would safely stay. So, each year my plastic animal family grew in my plastic rescue centre. I never believed one day my five hundred-piece toy farm set, a blueprint, would become a reality for the rescue centre, providing the most places of safety in the south east of England – a safe place for each species of my toy set and many more.

We all remember stories of animal lovers way back in our families but I'm lucky enough to remember two great uncles on my Nanny Glad's side who both loved animals. Uncle Ernie was the black sheep of the family, a free sprit known for his womanising. My memories of him are more different and when I was only seven my dad and I had to take a trip all the way from London to Somerset to 'sort Ernie's troubles out'. Unbeknown to me, Ernie was up to his old tricks again with the women and needed to leave town fast.

Dad and I arrived at the old farmhouse and had a look round for Ernie. Ernie knew we were coming, and I had heard my dad say to him on the phone before we left to be ready – and 'no trouble'. We pushed open the door and went into the ramshackle old house. Old Uncle Ern was an eccentric by anyone's standards, but my dad's face said it all. A donkey and goat in the kitchen were too much for my townie dad to stomach. We walked out and down the drive. It was still early for a Sunday morning, but Ernie was already out. My dad waved to a neighbour.

'We're here for Ernie,' he shouted. 'Any idea where he is?'

'Yes,' the neighbour shouted back. 'He's gone down the village shop for his papers.'

We waited until a smiling uncle Ernie came back up the drive not only with his Sunday papers but a following of his ducks and geese. Apparently, it was completely normal for Uncle Ern to visit the shop with donkey, goat or birds tagging on. I now know that Ernie was being thrown out; his womanising within the small village too much for his present girlfriend to stand. It was a very early dream of mine after this encounter to have a donkey and goat living in my kitchen and a long line of birds to follow me around Tesco.

One of Nanny Glad's other brothers was Charlie who was married to Hilda. Charlie and Hilda never had any children but devoted their time to helping stray dogs. They had many over the years and I always enjoyed my visit and the latest story of who they had helped. Benny, their latest rescue, was the craziest one ever and every day Hilda cooked him three meals a day, never anything from the tin. He had the best coat full of shine and beautiful bright eyes.

Aunty Hilda would also open her kitchen window and with crumbled up cheese she would call the wild birds. Her little whistle call of 'come on, come on' brought them all in. From blackbird to robin and starling and thrush she befriended them all. Such happy memories of a legacy of animal lovers.

CHAPTER TWO

SUBURBIA

By the time I was ten we were moving out of London to a family house in the suburbs. We would drive from the built-up streets of London and out to leafy Kent. Each day after school we excitedly travelled to decorate and refurbish the house and then at weekends we tried to tame the garden. Both direct neighbours were animal lovers and my excitement about our new life was hard to contain – I just wanted to move in.

One day when my dad was working on the garden, sweeping away, he called me to see what he had found in the sweepings.

'A lizard, a lizard!' he shouted, and we all crowded around a tiny dusty body. I picked her up out of the sweepings and cleaned her off. She was still alive. I marvelled at her lean body wondering how she got here. Where was she from? She had such tiny fingers and lay back exhausted in my hand. I safely put her in my pocket and returned with her to London. We had no idea she was not a lizard. We bought her a tank and all the set-up to keep her safe until we lived at the house when we would happily release her back into our garden.

We never thought it strange that our lizard was a water baby. The tank was on our window ledge and everyone on the council estate would stop and stare at our swimming lizard, an absolute highlight for most of the neighbours. Weeks later we found a second 'lizard' that we named Brian, who joined Lizzie. Our garden was alive with unimaginable wildlife, or so we thought. During a conversation with our neighbours a shocking discovery was uncovered: Brian and Lizzie were newts, and not lizards, as our very own South London David Attenborough had led us to believe.

Our new property, a 1930s semi-detached chalet house in Sidcup with a front and back garden was to become our prized home. My parents had worked hard to buy their first house and took such pride in making it our home. Both Mum and Dad had a strong work ethic and it was not unusual for both to have multiple jobs along with their own fledgling business. Our new home seemed like a mansion coming from the council flats of London and our own green space was like having a paddock. The house had a few fruit trees and a small pond which for me was an absolute dream come true. With privet hedges full of insects and birds I really believed we were now living in 'the sticks'.

The ancient woodlands of Shooter's Hill and epic public open spaces like Danson Park and Avery Hill park surrounded us. I was now closer to nature having left London and I was noticing more and more wildlife around me. My new school friends knew more about the types of birds and trees than I did but took it all for granted. Many had ponds in their gardens which they never looked in, and they didn't know which creatures called them home. Even the most common waterlily in our neighbour's pond was like finding the crown jewels for me, topped only by finding a newly formed frog the size of my little fingernail sitting on one.

My garden was my paradise, a real patch of Mother Nature and it wasn't long before I started to find little creatures to come and make it their home too. First was Pickles, the boss-eyed kitten that no one wanted due to a split personality, going from kindness to kill in three seconds. My dad, who was not that happy about living in Noah's ark, was the first to fall victim of Pickles. One night after a long night at work my dad slipped into bed naked as normal, only to stretch out and disturb the sleeping wild kitten under the sheets. Pickles grabbed his ankle with his front claws and pushed against his heel with back claws and then with no remorse bit into his toe. I remember my mum telling us that a swearing, naked Dad running around the house after a wild cat was not a happy Dad or a forgettable sight.

It soon became a regular nightly run of the gauntlet for my poor dad to meet my latest rescue in the early hours. My dad recalls coming home to find a pony sleeping in the front porch, an unwanted Great Dane, not happy to let him in at 1am and an early morning caller ringing our bell to be greeted by my exhausted dad.

'Is that your goat running down the road?' the caller had asked.

'I have no idea whether we have a goat or not, but most likely yes, knowing the family I live with,' my dad replied. There were no neighbours crazy enough to keep goats, so he was right. It was just like the TV series *The Good Life*, I hadn't had time to tell him that the goat I rescued now lived with us in suburbia.

Another time, my longest friend Daniele and her parents Del and Roger gave me a beautiful day-old duckling. Just the size of a tennis ball covered with soft yellow fluff, we named her Daffy. The new baby literally had to sleep with my mum in a small box on the bed and in the true style of our household when my dad returned late from work again, on slipping past the wild cat, amorous Great Dane and others, he made it to the safety of his bed. He must have thought things were getting easier on the Ark. The movement disturbed Daffy and she spotted him, jumped out of the box quacking and with her wet cold feet ran up and down his back and tried to bed down on his head.

My dad's impression of the Incredible Hulk never failed to amuse us, going from normal Dad to bursting point within minutes. There were so many last straws, but they turned into great after-dinner stories for when family and friends visited. If only my dad knew then that he was laying the foundation stones for such a pioneering project he may have been more accommodating; after all, he was captain of the Ark.

I had rescued a Shetland pony called Rickie, who slept in the front porch. Having originally been bought from a horse market, he was being given away due to contagious equine warts, so when we took him in he wasn't allowed in the stables where we kept our other ponies. To hide this one from Mum and Dad, my sister and I had to think on our feet and come up with plan B. Rather than waiting for our mum to arrive and be told off for getting yet another pony we would take him home. Unfortunately, we lived about six miles away from the stables and it would take us all evening to walk home.

'Don't worry,' I told my sister, 'we will get him on the bus.'
'How?' she replied.

I made her wait, or rather hide, in the bus shelter of the 132. On seeing the bus coming along I waved it down. I got on and asked with a smile on my face if we could bring on a large dog and the driver said yes, as long as we stood by the back doors. We quickly mounted the bus at the back doors and hoped no one would notice. *Please Rickie don't poo* both my sister and I pleaded with him. The two older ladies on the back of the bus found the whole situation delightful, asking his name and was he a pony? Lil and I talked about the ladies telling their families of a bus ride with a pony, wondering if anyone would believe them. We kept Rickie busy with mints and sugar cubes. We got off the bus leaving no clues that the public transport had been a horse lorry for a short while. The bus driver gave us a thumbs-up as he passed us.

My mum was working a shift in her newly acquired off license just along the road from the bus stop. I popped in ahead of Lil and Rickie and told my mum to close her eyes and accept our wonderful anniversary present for her and Dad. Before she opened her eyes, Rickie let out a massive neigh.

'You'd better be joking!' my poor mum shouted. With Rickie's big soft eyes and kind personality it didn't take long for both Mum and Dad to fall in love with him. They never really stopped being fascinated by what was next. They knew animals enriched all our lives and we were better off for sharing these incredible times with them. Rickie was now just one of many residents living in our suburban back garden. Rickie joined Nanny the goat, Dauphine (daffy) and Peter the ducks, Doublet the rabbit (who I had also brought home on a bus with school friend Rachel Cook), budgies, fifty-three gerbils, twelve tortoises, terrapins, fish, Rocky the Irish setter, Henry the Great Dane, Monty and Marmalade the ginger kitten twins and Charlie the Yorkshire terrier. My parents had to surrender eventually to my animal magnetism, even if at times they attempted a very firm 'absolutely not' and 'enough is enough'.

On one occasion our neighbour had abandoned their cat Samantha. She had been their pet since she was only weeks old. Samantha was an older mainly white cat with black spots, and was incredibly friendly and loving. My plan was to wait until a Sunday lunch-time session at the pub to ask my dad if we could take her in. This had worked for other ideas, although not usually animals. En route home when everyone was at their happiest after enjoying their favourite tipple, I brought up the plight of Samantha and explained in detail just how desperate the situation was. To my amazement my dad was the first to show his disgust at such behaviour.

'You bring that poor girl in straight away when we get home,' he said. Maybe today's session was slightly longer than normal, and the effects of extra beer had surprisingly worked in our favour. When we arrived back home we rushed to collect her from the alley.

There she was sitting by our gate. I scooped her up and, just like the time rescuing Mitzi at eight-years-old, I held her tight and made my way into the house. We made her comfortable in the dining room with a small bed and I felt so happy. She was now in the warm, we were all so grateful for Dad's kindness. Ever so quickly, I realised I may have got our new family member because Dad's decision-making was under the influence and when he woke up on Monday morning, he had a completely different attitude to having another cat. All the explaining that it was in fact Dad's decision did not change anything and he insisted that she went. 'Enough is enough, we don't need another cat' was Dad's standard line. We were heartbroken; in our eyes our home was a home for waifs and strays but for dad it was very different. We kept Samantha in the shed for a few days, and she remained a member of our household until my school friend took her home.

Our pony family also continued to grow with Lil's little pony Bess, a grey Connemara with a kind temperament, Tramp an unwanted cart horse with a laid-back disposition, Shady a crazy ex-racehorse and Flair, my heartbeat, a wilful New Forest that was the fastest thing on four legs. Each day after school when my sister and I would ride our ponies, my mum would walk with us accompanied by the dogs, goat and duck. Nobody could doubt that we were an animal-loving family, if not total eccentrics. Nothing stood in the way of our furry family growing month by month, not even Dad's 'enough is enough'.

On a romantic trip to Paris my parents left us in the capable hands of Nanny Glad. A great opportunity to grow the family came when I saw an advertisement in the local paper for 'new home wanted' for an Irish setter. Seeing as we already had Rocky, our loyal setter, I thought it might take a few days for the parents to realise there was now a second setter residing with us. I collected the sad setter from an animal hoarder's home and returned home with Boy Boy to join our menagerie. All went really well, and everyone loved each other and the two setters rushed around the house together playing like puppies.

With Rocky, our original setter, still sleeping by my parents' bed and Boy Boy, our new boy, happily sleeping in the kitchen, I thought how easy this had all been – but with their trip to Paris coming to an end, my parents would be home tomorrow. I had no time to hatch a plan. On arriving home with all the joys and excitement of seeing us and gift sharing in the hall, both my parents fussed Boy Boy thinking he was Rocky. We all went through to the kitchen where my dad commented on how fast 'Rocky' had got into the kitchen and we didn't even notice him passing us. Here Mum and Dad fussed Rocky again, or so they thought.

The next few hours were spent with my sister and I ensuring both dogs were not in the same room together, even taking one to the bathroom with me. It was inevitable that sooner or later, both dogs would end up in the same room and I would have some explaining to do. It wasn't long before everyone was in the lounge catching up, including the dogs. I saw my dad's face. Maybe he was thinking how very good that French red wine was because now he was seeing double? Time to explain and wait for the usual 'enough is enough'.

Our home may have been modest in size, but the heart was big. It was the social hub of our community, and family and friends were always there. It was a traditional old-school environment where neighbours popped in to borrow a cup of sugar or a few slices of bread. Where my school friends often hung out in our garden and never wanted to leave. What I couldn't get away with in the house, I would find space for in our shed, under my bed or at the stables.

My bedroom contained tanks of fish and terrapins and anything I could grow with my green fingers. My window ledge held plant pots of spider plants, cactus, bonsai, acorns and conkers pushed into little pots of peat, cuttings of anything green starting to root in water filled jam jars. This was the start of my plan to grow new forests for free. The creatures that the school keep in classrooms would often have young and I always volunteered to take them home. Anything born at school that wasn't perfect I would also sneak home and love. This always kept the occupancy of all areas full. Old discarded fish tanks doubled up as gerbil accommodation and stacked four high, males on the left and girls on the right. Rabbits lived in luxury, converted wardrobes and our other animals had the free roam of my dad's prized, green lush lawn.

One morning, Dad asked me to keep all pets off the lawn whilst he worked hard to perfect it for a forthcoming garden party, where he would entertain his rich and famous friends on my mini meadow. Two by two, I packed the residents of Noah's Ark into the garden shed so my dad could perform his miracle. The rest of the day, Dad sweated over the lawn mower, pulling up weeds and cutting back the privets, perfecting his masterpiece. A man's home is his castle after all, and this included the lawn. After hours of Dad's commitment to presenting our garden like something from the Chelsea Flower Show, he retired with a cold beer.

It wasn't long before the great breakout would overshadow all the day's hard work. Frustrated, Nanny the goat bashed down the door of Rescue Central with her impressive two-foot long horns to allow galloping pony, splashing ducks and pooing goat the freedom to ruin the Wimbledon lawn-lookalike. I very quickly disappeared on a walk with my four-legged friends and the two-legged quackers too. Dad eventually conceded defeat because the next episode was always just about to begin.

Nothing stood in the way of me saving animals and when I heard that pony owners at our stables were due to have their elderly pony shoot I pleaded to take them on. During my teens, most people around me knew I was the person to sort out any animal problem they came across. I knew every cat's name in the neighbourhood, happily played with all the dogs, knew where the fox had her cubs and when the first tadpoles would arrive. I would ride everyone's ponies and stood in between life and death of any animal who needed me.

At fourteen I became vegetarian after seeing dead wild rabbits in my Home Economics class. I happened to be friends with twins who were vegan, but I had never made the connection to loving animals, wanting justice for animal cruelty and still happily eating them. Seeing the limp lifeless beautiful bodies of innocent rabbits, just like those I kept safe at home, lying dead - a life ended all for a meal, helped the penny to drop loudly. It wasn't long until I noticed the rabbit fur trims on coats and lucky rabbit-foot key rings that had belonged to a creature who wanted to live. These animals had families and did no one any harm but still most kids didn't bat an eyelid at such injustices. Civilised society or cavemen wearing clothes? The hypocrisy didn't add up to me.

I extended my love for all things green when walking the dogs. I pushed acorns and other tree seeds into the ground where they dropped to help them survive and grow. I'm sure there's many new trees around Kent due to my legacy of seed-planting back in the day. My understanding even back then was what absolute assets trees were to us, the environment, and all those who lived and fed in them. I happily picked discarded litter up from a young age so not to endanger wildlife and would always ensure all leftover food made it to the woods to support the creatures living there during the winter. A nickname given to me back then was Earth Boy, which I always loved. After all, I loved everything that belonged to nature. I was at my best in the garden with the animals or planting something here and there. I suppose even then I was always an environmentalist at heart. The start of my journey for a kinder, more compassionate world as an animal activist had now started.

Throughout my late teens I slowly but surely rescued more and more animals, from straying sheep to unwanted rodents, street cats and dogs, ex-racehorses, pet goats, chickens, pigeons even an unwanted, retired police horse. The numbers of creatures reliant on me was rapidly growing fast. Animals just seemed to find me, to talk to me and of course asked for my help. How could I say no?

A favourite saying of mine is 'animals do speak but only to those who know how to listen'. I was always listening. It wasn't unusual for me to set off to London by train to go clubbing, visit museums, art galleries or the ballet and party up town, only to return back home with a sick pigeon or two from Trafalgar Square to join my twenty-plus at home before I even got to the destination. Frustrated mates who only wanted to get on with whatever today's experience was, had me coordinating a pigeon rescue now.

On a visit to The National Gallery with friends, I spotted a young swan wandering around Trafalgar Square and knowing he could not take off, I immediately set about planning to help him find his way home. With the help of my reluctant friends who just wanted an afternoon of culture and not animal rescue, we slowed and stopped the traffic so our feathered friend could cross the road. I walked him off the square, with Nelson on his column watching over us and then over and through Admiralty Arch on to the Royal Mall and through to the lake on St James's park. My embarrassed friends pointing out the smiles on people's faces on the tourist buses and one angry driver who shouted out 'get a dog like everyone else!' made it all worthwhile.

On another occasion in London, I tried to befriend a homeless man and give him some food for his sad-looking dog. I had spotted the man being unkind to his dog and just wanted to see if I could help. I introduced myself calmly with the offer of food for both of them.

'Just take her,' the man said to my surprise, and aggressively walked off.

The hungry little collie-cross still wanted her human but hunger took over and she ate the pasty and smiled lovingly at me, her tail wagging. Back into Victoria station I went with Tara, the dog from the homeless man, only to then find a sad-looking pigeon baby on the ground, so the three of us returned home on the train, missing my friend's eighteenth birthday party. Tara settled into what she must have seen as a life of luxury with a sea of dog beds, endless dog treats, blankets and comfy well-chewed chairs.

Veganism had followed me for a few years, raising its ethical head and getting me to question my stand on eggs and dairy. Was it really cruel? Could I carry on eating such things?

My vegan friends, or the 'vegang' as I called them gave me the evidence, but I just couldn't believe the omelettes, ice cream and cheese I loved so much could be so cruel to the animals and birds producing them. My belief that chickens and cows happily laid eggs and produced milk for us was about to come to an end.

Ignorance was not bliss it was in fact the relationship with all animals that comes with becoming vegan that is true bliss. It was a journey of self-enlightenment and an inner decision to do less harm. The 'V' conversation came up again so I said I would do my own research. I went along to the library on Monday and collected five books, which seemingly contained all the answers – after all, library books don't lie. I read the idyllic books of farming, about how the farmer and his wife loved the animals that made them rich. Of course they weren't just commodities. How could they be? They're just big dogs and as a nation we love dogs. These animals had everything they wanted including names. Kind and happy names like Buttercup, Clover, Rosie and Daisy implied a kind of soft and gentle world that these animals lived in.

The fact the books showed no old cattle or hens in retirement went over my head because these books presented a glossy, animal paradise with no room to suspect that the family farm was not a kind and loving place, with animals happily giving us their products. After all, if the farmer looked so happy and loved his animals, who was I to look further than the pages of *Life on the Farm* and *From Farm to Fork*. The fact that the books were published by the meat, dairy and egg industries all profiteering from turning a blind eye still hadn't dawned on me, but these books were as much

31

fiction as the *Doctor Who* novels on the other shelves.

The second conversation that week with the vegang resulted in them offering me a trip to a dairy farm behind their aunty's house down in the depths of Kent. I agreed because after all a day in the country hanging out with cattle seemed like pure Disney after reading the cows-in-paradise library books. When we set off to visit the farm I never for one moment thought I would be disappointed with my day out, so the outcome of the day was a complete and utter surprise to me.

Arriving at the vegang's aunty's home I breathed the fresh air of the Kent countryside and immediately felt relaxed. Everyone was excited to see each other and kisses of joy were exchanged at the front door. Rooty the cocker spaniel showed an additional interest in me, probably because I smelled more like a dog than he did. We settled on the patio of the back garden. Seated at the large table in the shade of the apple tree, I thought about how nice it would be living a more country life. Lemonade, beer, crisps, jam rolls, fruit and cashew nuts had all been laid on the table for the travellers to feast on. Aunty Jean was old hat at feeding the vegang when they visited even if she wasn't vegan herself.

The house was surrounded by open fields and bright blue skies with not a cloud to be seen. The fields were full of black and white cows happily chewing the cud. The silence was breathtaking, only broken by the occasional moo and distant cuckoo. I thought to myself what a beautiful day and just how lucky was Aunty Jean to live in such paradise. I had my fair share of lemonade and worked my way over the table of treats and by this time I started to tell a few of my famous favourite jokes. Knowing my jokes, the vegang moved quickly to get me out of earshot of Aunty Jean and suggested we go to meet the cows.

We walked across the green, lush fields stopping to greet the gentle cattle one by one. Some showed some interest in us and others were reserved. Each one had such hope in their eyes, hope for us despite all we do to them. Their natures were so generous to us despite our failings, absolutely no judgement for the crimes carried out against them. We climbed the fence into the farmyard and called out to Mike the farmer.

The farmhouse was beautiful, a real dream home and it stood in its own mature garden. The garden was full of shrubs and colourful flowers everywhere. Climbing up the house and across the front was the most beautiful wisteria with hanging flowers like I'd never seen before. The many pollinators worked hard collecting from it and I could hear a steady buzz of happiness. The front door opened and two mad sheepdogs came running out to greet us. Hunny and Peter barked and ran around us and with shiny coats and eyes they looked so well looked after.

This picture of idyllic union between man and beast would surely include the cattle, wouldn't it? We were taken around the farm to meet the cattle who were in. I was first introduced to a group of cows eating away at the silage, seemingly happy. Then I was asked if I wanted to see the nursery and my smiles said it all – of course, who wouldn't want to see baby animals, especially cute calves?

The nursery was in fact rows of barren metal pens and in each one a tiny, sad and scared-looking calf. In the dark miserable barn these babies stood in veal crates without a single comfort. I felt sick and heartbroken for each terrified new-born. I gently leant over to touch the face of one beautiful creature and he started to suckle my fingers, his dry mouth desperate for his mother's milk and his eyes betraying a horrid story. I will never forget the moments of comfort he got from this. If these were puppies or foals, the country would be up in arms and rightly so. These babies meant nothing to the farmers. They were forgotten and our system had failed them. They were just lumps of meat, not living breathing creatures.

How cruel and barbaric in this day and age to cause such upset, all hidden away behind a mask of happiness. All those calves needed was their mums. I felt so terrible to have looked the other way for so long, to have ignored one simple step to move my thoughts feelings and action in line with each other to become kind and to catch up with my own moral compass.

'Six weeks 'til they're on your plate,' someone said. Mortified, I turned to face the farmer.

'How do you get these babies to drink water from a bucket?' I asked him.

'A welly to the head,' he replied with no emotion. When the calves are put in the crates the farmer walks along forcing the heads of the crying babies into the buckets by stepping on their heads and holding them under the fluid. Needless to say, from this day onwards I was a fully paid-up member of the vegang and have never looked back.

During the 1990s after I sadly lost Joe, the then love of my life, I needed new challenges. I could either give up or pull my socks up and rebuild myself. What good is a heap of emotions to anyone? My quest for kindness took me to many places in the world with adventures near and far, luxurious and cheap. From planes trains and automobiles, I either backpacked or travelled in style depending on my host at the time. There was always a story of adventure to tell, many still too early to give back life to. There's enough stories of my rescue antics to fill another book and with my animal rescue life at home being as busy as my full-time employment and relationships I always knew my life with animals would make me more like a real-life Doctor Dolittle or Ace Ventura Pet Detective. The only difference was that this was real, and I had more animals.

CHAPTER THREE

PUTTING ROOTS DOWN

By the time I was in my early twenties, I was living in a flat at the top of a large Victorian house in Blackheath, South East London. The flat had no mod cons, no TV, no microwave, no central heating but a million books, just how I liked it. Those books and many others still share my life today. The large, open fireplace in my bedroom often saw the heavy fog that settled on the heath come down the chimney and settle in the flat. I would wake up to a freezing, hazy fog happily hanging out over my bed. I often had friends staying for months on end and it was a highlight to many people's life, sharing in just a few of the many rescues.

My family of rescued animals and plants had grown exponentially and now it included sheep, goats, horses of all shapes and sizes, eleven dogs, thirty-seven cats, ninety rodents, pigeons, and a one-winged sparrow called Mighty who lived in the branches of the huge plants that graced the lounge. Of course, the large mammals didn't live many floors up with me; they had some fields just outside of London, although many did spend time being nursed in the flat including lambs, goats and the odd foal. It wasn't unusual for me to be relaxing on the second-hand sofa that had seen better times with bottle-feeding foal, disabled birds, an array of moggy misfits and serval canine delinquents. In fact, some of my best evenings were spent on that sofa where I worked hard to save a new rescue. I would sometimes spend all night on there, nursing a creature back to health and waking up with a stiff neck and a new-born foal asleep on top of me.

My evenings took me around London trapping feral cats and getting them an MOT, as we called it. A cat MOT was having their eyes and ears checked and cleaned, anti-parasite treatment, and being neutered and microchipped. The majority were returned to their original location with a feeder in place to support the cats. Some feral cat sites had up to seventy cats living on them. I would single-handedly fund everything, from referral veterinary costs to quarantine, making sure these animals had everything they needed.

Pretty much every penny I've ever earned has gone into my rescue work. Usually my kind and supportive partner would cover my living costs, knowing my salary were only there to support needy animals. Long before the internet came along my home phone would ring day and night with messages of help needed for injured wildlife, abandoned dogs and starving horses. My little black Fiat Uno was an unofficial animal ambulance and would bring home injured deer, wild birds, feral cats to see the vet the following day, tens of angry kittens to tame and find homes for at any one time, sick and starving street dogs needing a warm bed to recover. If my car failed to fit the patient, I would borrow my sister Lil's bigger car to assist absolutely any creature in need of my help. Most times I wouldn't confess to her that with the backseat laid down, I brought home a weak and starving pony in the back of her pride and joy. I'm sure if she had known she would not have cared.

I became the 24/7 unofficial rescuer for London who never slept. No uniform or salary from animal welfare, just my commitment to those who needed me most. My rescue work also included humanely trapping rats from people's homes and finding them happy and safe release sites and clearing buildings due for demolition of pigeons and other nesting birds. In the times before Health and Safety, I would clamber up ladders with my tools, baskets and anything I needed to save the babies entrusted to me.

Rescue sites included railway bridges, empty high-rises of all shapes and sizes and boardwalks over the River Thames. Then there were the scores of tethered horses who, whatever the weather, had no shelter, no rugs, no hay and no water. I would drive around dropping piles of hay, water tubes and food to see them through the night. I watched many give birth at the end of a ten-foot rope and found many perished bodies too. This heart-breaking mission is still needed today.

Those early horses I visited knew the sound of my engine and greeted me with a whinny. On occasions a horse was surrendered to me due to her no longer giving birth, or because her health was poor. An emergency operation would then commence, removing the horse before the owner changed his mind and the poor soul would freeze to death in the night. Usually I'd drive to find a friend who was free to do the transport and beg their support. One friend, Horse-Lorry Pauline, was always up for a rescue and helped me save so many desperate horses.

Thankfully it wasn't long before mobile phones became available and what a help they were, even if people ignored my name when ringing in the early hours. My nightly rescue team of helpers included serval of the dogs who could not be left at home, others who loved their dad so much and just enjoyed the company, and nearly always Bev the broiler chicken who I had had from a day old and was inseparable from. I would happily drive into the night with a dachshund across my shoulders another two on my lap. The passenger seat easily squeezed three on and in the footwell was Bev's bed.

The loft may have been rather large accommodation but for my ever-growing family I desperately needed more space. My doorbell would ring throughout the night by local animal lovers who had found an injured animal or their own animal needed help. I was so lucky to have the kindness and support of a few very kind vets in the days before the multinationals swallowed up the independent veterinary clinics and a banker decided people helping animals was detrimental to the company's bank balance.

One such vet was Phillip Parker of Sidcup Veterinary Centre. Phillip was instrumental in helping me help the many animals that came along. He was very sympathetic to my vision and never cornered me even when my account reached £10,000. In fact, he was a gentleman who always thanked me for eventually paying my bill. He was also the first vet to offer me a 20% discount on all work done by him. I happily in return took home injured wildlife and unwanted pets left at his surgery.

An easy breakdown of my living arrangements was on entering the flat, the kitchen and lounge was for most of the dogs usually about ten dogs, including Lovejoy and Blissful, two adorable dachshunds who came from puppy farms, Eden and Eva, lively and excitable ex-hunting lurchers and an assortment of blind and deaf dogs with other medical needs like diabetes, heart failure and epilepsy. There were also resident cats like Straussymousy-rubberlegs, a little white fluffy cloud, Augustus Gloop and Sebastian Braveheart. The cats had an outside runway from my old Victoria sash kitchen window down to ground zero to access the garden. An assortment of ramp-style boards with treads on to stop them slipping in the rain ensured the cats could come and go as they pleased day or night.

The bathroom and back bedroom housed rodent accommodation and new arrival and hospital cages. Penelope Pipstop, the sweetest, largest, female rat you had ever seen who I had hand-reared now lived loose in the bathroom. Formerly a wild orphan, she arrived via a neighbour after her cat carried her in. She was hairless and had her eyes still closed. This little pip turned out to be a larger-than-life character. The hallway, with its small roof window for free flying pigeons, was often frequented by the odd blackbird or starling after a free meal. The top hallway and bedrooms mainly housed feral cats and larger short-stay mammals.

The flat also housed my collection of gigantic plants of all types. Plants being my second love, I would acquire them from everywhere – not just cuttings or seeds, but also six-foot yuccas left outside office buildings, which I would bring home to bring back to life.

Many of my four-legged flat sharers were so old they spent their lives cuddled up in 'snuggle pads' and in the makeshift skyscrapers of beds I would make for them. The airing cupboard remained open and the shelves of the linen became bunk beds for cats long past their expiry dates. Each shelf had a water bowl and luxury bowl of food tucked away, just like breakfast-in-bed-come-room-service.

Having basically a library, farmyard and rainforest in an apartment was never easy, even if it was fun and full of love for the many residents. Thirty-seven litter trays, one for each of the cats and wee-wee towels for the old and incontinent dogs made the summer the worst months. I tried everything to stop the dogs from peeing on the floorboards and it pouring through the downstairs celling and on the occasions that it did make it through, I would blame the worn-out old pipes of Victorian plumbing. Avoiding odours was no easy task and constant juggling of mop and bucket, piles of hand-washed towels, toilet rolls and anything that could mask the potent smells of life in the loft. Then there was the invasion of flies that somehow could outsmart me at every level. Never one to even kill a fly, I tried everything from pots of lavender, mint plants, lemon water in tea-light jars and burning anti-insect joss sticks inside the loft. In the end, I admitted defeat and lived with a very impressive swarm.

One occasion my flat mate 'Shotgun Jonnie' answered the door and let in a bailiff. He was looking for a previous tenant, but Shotgun thought he was seeking help in animal rescue. The pushy and arrogant bailiff made his way up the stairs asking for Mr Black. I explained with crow on my shoulder there was no one by that name here, unless one of my fluffy flat mates had a surname of Black and he would need to try elsewhere. The bailiff ignored my advice, flashing his card and opening the door to a Pandora's box of sleeping ankle-biters.

'I wouldn't go in there,' I shouted, but it was too late. With what I'm sure felt like a thousand shark's teeth tearing at his flesh through his trousers and shoes, he tried his hardest to get out of the geriatric ward for tiny antisocial canines.

'The more you struggle the more they bite,' I called to him. 'Just try and stay still, stay calm and stop screaming!'

This is easier said than done when tiny pins are ripping at your flesh. Even the oldies with no teeth were doing their best to restrain the stranger. Sadly, then the chap in a bid to escape fell down the first stairwell with an assortment of breeds of dogs hanging onto his leg. It was like mob rule and not even I could intervene. On trying to recover his position he placed a hand on a shelf where I had a rescue station, a jar lid of sugar water for worn-out wasps using the pigeon window as a drive-through. Just before I could warn him of the resting lethal patients, the tiniest of creatures gave him the biggest sting. He must have thought the flat was booby-trapped to the highest level. Twisting and turning, sucking his hand, he quickly made it down more stairs. He eventually freed himself of the jaws of my protectors and left the building shaken, index finger-throbbing and needing new trousers, but hopefully only his pride was bruised.

All in a day's work, I thought to myself, and wrote him a poem.

CHAPTER FOUR

THE EXPANSION

With the loft full to bursting point, my sister came up with the clever idea of expanding my set-up to the derelict property next door. Sadly a few years before, my neighbour Joseph (John) had died. John had lived at number 71 for more than sixty years. He and his brother lived alone after they lost their fiancées during the war and remained heartbroken. Just after the great storm of 1987 John's brother died and left John, who was already a recluse, alone. I accidentally befriended John one summer's evening after he shouted out of an upstairs window for help. He was already blind, frail and in his eighties. I had assumed the house was empty when I moved in because it was falling into disrepair. I hung out my upstairs window and called out to him.

'Who's that?' he shouted.

'It's Billy, your neighbour,' I called back.

Someone was breaking into his house on the ground floor. I immediately summoned my gang of obliging canines to the rescue, most of whom only lived to sink their teeth into someone's flesh. We stormed into our back garden and through the gate into next door's overgrown jungle. We came face-to-face with two guys about twenty years old, holding a carriage clock and a picture, climbing out of a broken downstairs window. Upon seeing us, the pair dropped everything and took off down into the undergrowth, thinking they had outsmarted me because I didn't know the layout.

Sadly for them, my dogs would outrun them and enjoy the hunt. To the screams of 'it's biting me' and 'get your dogs off me', I couldn't help but smile and think, *well they won't listen to me*. I eventually called my bodyguards back. One dog called Chip returned with a large patch of tracksuit in her mouth.

I called up to John and told him they had gone, and he thanked me. I had lived at the flat for some months and this was our first meeting. He pushed open the old patio door and manoeuvred the years of cluttered protection. We shook hands, a rather odd introduction but a powerful one. I handed him his belongings back and we chatted for a while. Break-ins to John's house, I was told, were a regular problem.

This handshake was the start of a short-lived but great friendship of five years. John had no family and no surviving friends, and he never left his house for anything. A charity volunteer did his shopping every week but never stayed to chat with him. He was all alone and never got to talk to anyone other than communicating what he wanted in his shopping. I was honoured when, the evening after our first meeting, I was invited in the following week which lead to a weekly meet. Every week we got together in John's for a morning chat and a guaranteed laugh. He'd led an amazing, talented life before heartache took most of him away. Once a celebrated animator for *Punch* magazine and an amateur photographer, the cruelty of losing his sight locked him away. I would now take over his shopping and treat him to something new each week. I would read him the papers and have a little tidy up. I'd put his rubbish out and make sure he had everything he wanted.

My greatest discovery was that John's garden had actually won awards and slowly through the weeds I could see the shape and structure of what was once his pride and joy. He showed me photos of his garden, of the local boxing matches he fought in and the parade of circus animals that came to town right past our front door. Occasionally he would give me one of his treasured books, which I still have to this day.

The yobs that broke in that day will never know what an amazing outcome came from their act of petty, miserable crime. Their only memories will be the teeth marks of my darling dogs sunk deep into their shady flesh. A surprise friendship that transcended the generations. John was a gentleman of a lost time and a very special friend. The second surprise was my collection of unwanted mutts assured there would never be another break in. Any late-night noises outside and their haunting howling would start.

Sadly our friendship came to a sudden end when I found John had passed away one night; how I missed our weekly chats and his wisdom. We talked about everything and although our views on many topics were so different, our friendship of serendipity could weather any disagreement or in John's words, 'we'll beg to differ on that one then'.

John's passing left an empty house five times the size of my flat. Not much planning was needed before John's home was accommodating different animals and birds on each level. My reputation for taking in any animal at any hour really needed this expansion. The top floor was for birds including the rehabilitation of crows, magpies and jackdaws from the local Greenwich Park, then a small room with free flying aviary birds. The next rooms were for swans and the occasional Canada geese who strayed from the heath onto the road. The next level was isolation for cats followed by a whole floor for rabbits who loved getting under the floorboards and living life like in the warren. A maternity ward of two linking rooms was next. A chicken and turkey room complete with heat lamps that looked out on to the garden from the first floor. The ground floor was for the unusual guest, peacocks, pony, goat, wallabies, emus and Pops the American skunk. The cellar was for recovering foxes and clubs. Every inch an animal hospital and a static Noah's Ark. The many free newspapers posted through the letter box every week were received with thanks and used to line litter trays or floor covers in the bird rooms.

We covered the front windows behind the curtains with cardboard, furniture and anything that would not expose our little urban secret. Since John had no living next of kin or had made a will, his estate fell to the government's Treasury Department. Thankfully, it takes years to sort out the necessary paperwork and relative searches, and our covert animal rescue centre was fully operational there for nearly two years. Grateful thanks must go to an unsung hero of animal rescue who accidentally after death loaned his home to us to lay the foundations of The Retreat, thank you John.

CHAPTER FIVE

THE FLIES

Animal rescue was a great way of judging potential lovers' compassion. Compassion is not something you can fake or turn on and off. It is a deep-rooted emotion and for me the most attractive quality in a person, and a lack of compassion is just plain ugly. You're either compassionate or not; you can't care about one animal and not another and think you're compassionate.

Although I've only ever been truly loved in my relationships, many were not long-term suitors; more lover than husband material. Animal rescue is emotionally draining, physically exhausting, financially ruining, it's filled with highs and lows and it's not for the faint-hearted. The last thing an animal rescuer needs is someone clingy and needy, who competes for attention and can't celebrate your calling. It's hard work, where days turn into nights and nights turn into days with very little sleep in between and somehow your other life of career, family and relationships is in there somewhere too. Another responsibility is not what a rescuer needs. You only have so much love to give so if someone is needing your undivided attention it won't last. Strong, independent types are best and usually being career-driven helps because they will understand your passion, your drive, your energy and of course my famous line, 'sorry I'm late (again)'.

I have many hilariously funny dating stories but for now I'll stick to my favourite one. Once upon a time, I was young, fit and eligible. I even had hair on my head and not growing out of my ears and nose and then there was a waistline too. My energy and zest for life was unmatched and I was unaware this was hugely attractive to those I was mixing with; I was oblivious to the interest I got unless you talked animal.

I would attend any function near or far, home or abroad that I was invited to and this produced so many more opportunities, including meeting some people on their way to stardom. I learnt very quickly that one good opportunity often leads to another, and this in turn has led me down the beautiful path life's given me.

Andrew was an intellect and from a well-to-do traditional Greek family. He was tall, dark and handsome. Andrew had lived a happy life and enjoyed the finer things in life – and then along I came. We were roughly the same age as each other and we hit it off immediately. We never would have met if it wasn't for me turning up at a friend's house on the off chance he was in. Andrew and I left together and walked to the tube. I found his poems intriguing and romantic and him finding my jokes (by the look on his face) rather shocking, our friendship was born.

He was very mature for his age and I was the Peter Pan of life never wanting to grow up. We spent long hours on the phone philosophising about life and finding ways of disappearing for afternoons. As much as we enjoyed each other's company and had a strong forever friendship, the relationship did not have a future and we both knew that. We would meet for dinner and walk in the London parks afterwards enjoying the night sky and the moon reflecting on the lakes. We both loved the architecture of London, especially at night. The many London bridges lit up would be a treat to drive over together. A few times we met for lunch too and I would talk animals and he would talk art and business.

On one occasion, we met for dinner near where I lived, and I struggled to get out of the whole 'can I come back for coffee and meet the animals?', knowing that what was behind the door of my flat may be too much for him. There would be a million mouths to feed and a ton of poop to clear up, not to mention that the flies would be enough to kill any romantic interest for sure. I tried my hardest to send him on his way, but Andrew was not taking no for an answer.

'There's something I need to tell you before we go in,' I told him when we arrived at the front door to my flat. A howling gang of wolves in the background happy to hear their dad was home was the least of my worries. Just how would I explain the flies to Greece's version of Little Lord Fauntleroy? I took a deep breath.

'Listen,' I went on. 'You know I love animals?'

'Yes, I do,' he replied excitedly. 'Come on, what is it?'

'Look, there's something else I must tell you, there's something I rescue and you may not understand. Insects – well, flies,' I lied. 'I get calls to collect injured flies some who are so injured it takes time for them to recover and fly again.' The love was disappearing from his eyes as the realisation of what I was telling him sunk in.

'That's fine, I'm sure,' he said, slightly puzzled but being an absolute gentleman. Was he trying to work out if something was lost in translation, despite speaking better English than I did? Did I really mean flies?

We entered the flat. The door opened onto a stairwell which we needed to climb but this was the night-time resting spot for the casualties of fly rescue.

'Try not to disturb them,' I said. Sneaking past, we only disturbed a few who flew off to higher ground. Then came the questions: 'Who calls you for injured flies? How far will you travel for an injured fly? What do you collect them in? Do they just get on with the others?'

I gracefully answered each question, thinking we would never need to discuss it again. I cleared away the thrown-up cat biscuits from a chair in the kitchen and Andrew sat down. Clearly shocked by the level of creatures sharing my life I made him that coffee. Was this coffee really what he thought it would be?

We wandered into the lounge to meet the next group of misfits and I quickly removed the wee-wee towels with some pressies from the dogs on. I smiled at Andrew, who was being mobbed by a pack of interested hounds, clearly overwhelmed by this level of puppy love. Libby the resident Shetland pony stood up from her sleeping position, whilst Romeo and Juliet, the lovebirds, drank the tea I'd left on the side. We enjoyed a few hours chatting, laughing and chilling with the farmyard and I truly thought that would be the last I'd see of Andrew romantically. His taxi arrived to take him home and we said goodnight.

As I shut the front door, I thought to myself what a different world it is out there to the sanctuary of my flat. My flat was a safety net for so many creatures who had struggled in the real world, the real world was cruel. Behind the red door lay a world of peace and harmony and to my surprise Little Lord Faultlroy seemed to enjoy his visit.

When I answered the phone the next day to Andrew, I was taken aback that he even called. His excited voice seemed to remember names of the deadliest of my residents and even still laughed at a joke I told. What a lovely evening it was and he couldn't wait to see me again and would I join him at an important function arranged by his family at a swanky London hotel. He didn't mention the flies at all so I relaxed, assuming he had forgotten. Never one to turn down an invitation I excitedly said yes.

We continued to enjoy each other's company in the build-up to his big event. The day of the function arrived and on the evening of the party I did my best with a new suit, £12 from a charity shop, clean underpants and socks and I even dusted my shoes. Looking dapper and not smelling of horse manure or cat pee, I set off to enjoy my evening. I had promised not to show any romantic signs in front of family and guests, and he assured me that I could just be myself and everyone would love me.

Andrew pointed out the who's who of the guest list and I started to feel a little underdressed. The glass of wine I was drinking probably cost more than my suit. Everyone was well dressed and important. Soon we were seated, and I sat opposite a very fine lady. Their titles didn't mean much to me; I would never remember Lady Whoever sitting next to Lord What's-His-Name. Andrew sat on the opposite side to me, three people down. My strange plate of starters arrived just before the others.

'What are you eating there?' Lady Whoever said. I couldn't work out what it was but realising it was just some sort of grated vegetable arranged like a piece of modern art. I just opened my mouth to reply, 'it's just vegetables,' when Andrew lent across.

'Billy is an animal rescuer,' he announced proudly. 'He takes this ethos very seriously. He even rescues flies up to a hundred miles from his home. He receives calls at all sorts of hours, he rushes out with his rescue pack of matchboxes for hospital beds and brings them home to recover in a designated flight just inside his own front door for those injured flies.'

The guests listened with puzzled looks on their faces. I've never been so embarrassed – how would I tell him that was a joke? Andrew continue the conversation with the people sitting directly next to him and they continued to look over at me. The rest of the guests, bewildered by meeting a real-life fly rescuer, ate their food in silence, probably wondering why anyone would go to such lengths to save flies when most people sitting at the table happily shot, fished and hunted anything and everything. It wasn't long until they could escape the table to tell others of their odd encounter with a man who saves all creatures, including flies. Andrew came over and smiled at me, and I half-smiled back, wishing I hadn't lied. He told me how interested people were in my work, and how proud he was of what I did for all animals, including flies.

Many weeks later whilst on a dog walk with Andrew and the hounds of Blackheath, I gently told him that the fly rescue story was a joke, an excuse for living with so many flies and how sorry I was he thought it true. By the look on his face he was actually disappointed I didn't travel hundreds of miles to rescue flies.

CHAPTER SIX

A BUILDER'S TALE

On a beautiful quiet summer's evening I took the opportunity for a good long soak in a bubble bath. In true gay style, with Barbara Streisand's *Guilty* playing loud and an eclectic collection of scented candles burning, I settled down to unwind without a worry in the world. I was accompanied by a very large whiskey, serval of the dogs trying to eat the bubbles and cats in the sink cleaning themselves and on the toilet seat judging the dogs on wasting their energy.

I relaxed into the deep hot water. Even in the bad light, it wasn't long before I noticed some odd patches of darkness in the plaster on the walls. I had only noticed the patches because my feet were up by the taps where my darling Penelope Pipstop the rat was resting. I was keeping a close eye on her to make sure she didn't drop into the water. I savoured the time and made the most of my restful evening.

When bath time was over and Streisand had sung her last, 'Woman in Love', I got out the bath and evacuated the occupants. I quickly dried myself and investigated the patches. I had no idea what the problem was, but the patches were damp and the wall was crumbling. The thought of having to have a builder in was as scary as bringing Andrew home on our date. Where could I put all the creatures of the loft if work needed doing? The best I could do was shut off all rooms and hope for the best. The absolute horror if a surveyor had to come in and the mystery of the lost Noah's Ark was exposed. Thankfully I could find no other patches of damp throughout the flat, although I was no expert. I was given a builder's number and hoped it could be sorted soon so the secret life of animal rescue would carry on uninterrupted.

The chosen builder couldn't come at a time when I was home, so I spoke with Angela, who lived downstairs and agreed to let him in. I gave the dogs an extra walk that day and even managed a bit more of a clean-up. All doors were shut off with signs stuck on them clearly stating NO ENTRY. I left happily, confident that nothing could go wrong.

On arrival, the builder was directed to the bathroom by Angela. Whilst he inspected the oddly shaped, poorly converted bathroom, he realised that the problem seemed to lead to behind the bath. Whilst lying on the floor and unscrewing the bath panel in the small space, he came across a terrifying unexpected problem, one no builder could fix. Removing the panel, he then pulled himself under the bath to further investigate the problem.

It was at this point that Penelope Pipstop must have been disturbed. Her bolt-hole down the back of the taps to under the bath was her sanctuary away from the madness of the other residents. I would watch her carry bedding of toilet tissue, face flannels and midnight treats such as grapes and walnuts down to her home. Penelope was so tame, so friendly, and just like a tiny dog she loved everyone, so without a second of hesitation she leaped onto the stranger's shoulder. In that terrifying moment, he jumped up and tried to retreat but bashed his head on the bath above. His shouts for help only resulted in Penelope Pipstop reaching up to kiss and hold his face. He rolled from under the bath and in a Linford Christie-style sprint made it out of the flat.

'Rising damp is only the start of your problems,' he shouted to Angela, 'you're infested with giant attack rats!'

This was not in a day's work for most people, so I really had some making up to do. I called Dick the builder and invited him back with sincerest apologies. Under my wing, he met the offender who had seen him off. She was no sabre-toothed tiger after all but a very laid-back, friendly rodent. He picked up Penelope Pipstop and immediately loved her. Dick and his family were kind animal lovers and he became our regular plumber and builder who the residents of the flat learned to love. His family also became foster homes for my overflow of rejects. He never failed to turn up with builder bags of treats for everyone. His first visit to the flat was enough to have put anyone off but this became his favourite work story and the start of his love affairs with Penelope Pipstop.

Dick's second famous story also happened at the flat and turned out to be not so rewarding. I had been having terrible problems with blocked drains in the flat. The old Victorian downpipes five floors up were not coping with me flushing the contents of litter trays and wee-wee towels down the pan. Dick was working hard on ladders outside trying to find the problem. He dismantled many runs of the downpipes and on shouting to me to put the kettle on. I walked off to make his coffee, but missed the second and most important part of his message: 'Don't flush anything until I say so'.

I made him his usual coffee with five sugars and handed it

out the nearest window to him with the usual warning about what those five sugars were doing to his teeth. Off down the ladder he went for a well-earned break. I carried on with the cleaning and emptied Hank and Storm's litter trays into the toilet to clear away the nasty evidence that they suffered from irritable bowel syndrome. Without another thought I pulled the chain and flushed away the daily ablutions of the cats. Within seconds I heard Angela shout 'Oh my God!' and Dick shout out 'I told him not to flush!'.

I slowly leaned out of the window and in a scene straight out of a *Carry On* movie I could see Dick completely covered top to toe and still holding his cup of coffee in his hand with Hank and Storm's IBS litter tray remains dripping off him. I quietly slipped out the front door before I was hung, drawn and quartered and went shopping for yet another apology gift.

CHAPTER SEVEN

TEACHING KINDNESS

My favourite job throughout my working time was the one of nursery schoolteacher. It never felt like work. Children naturally love animals and never want to harm anything living, so for me it was a match made in heaven. The lessons I taught were on friendship, nature and kindness; I would teach my class to harm no living thing, not even a fly (you can ask Andrew about that one).

Most days we spent hours in the garden working under the shade of huge London plane trees, judging the time by where the sun was. We saved tiny creatures in the garden and built them the very first bug houses and hotels. We had bird feeding stations and knew where our resident snails spent the day, stuck to the fence deep inside the ivy. Our highlights were the weekly trips out to Greenwich Park to visit the deer and feed the ducks, pigeons and squirrels. My nature class loved the freedom and it was the easiest part of their learning. Every single lesson can be taught outside in a natural classroom simply using nature. Children feel more at home outside than in the classroom so they are able to focus and learn more. Nature calms them and they enjoy the breeze and good light.

One high point of my teaching job was when we went on a school trip to a farm-park project. This I knew would bring some disappointing human factors to the awareness of my class. Here we would see an 'us and them' scenario between those of us who saw animals as being just like us and those who were indifferent to their plight. I wanted my class to know that these animals we called 'farm animals' were actually just animals like the dogs and cats that shared our homes and hearts. I could show my class there was a kinder route in life, one that didn't compromise our true values like freedom and kindness. Maybe the children were too young to know that slaughterhouses were not holiday camps for animals, but I could point them in the right direction to know how kind choices could make a positive impact on animals.

Our trip to the farm-park resulted in my little people making such an important decision all by themselves. Their reactions and actions shocked me; maybe I had underestimated them all. On our afternoon walk around the farm-park we had noticed an older sheep in a pen by herself. My inquisitive class began asking questions: *Why is she alone? What's her name? Where are her friends?* The animal carer replied that she had no name and that the farm was finished with her. He went on to say that she was blind, and that the following week she would be off to market. The children continued with their questioning. *Market? Can we give her a name?*

This was where my plastic farm-set training came into play. I saw the faces on my class change when they realised the market was not like the one they visited with their families but an end of life market. Now they turned to each other with their ideas on how to find her another home. My class decided this was too sad and asked if we could bring her back to nursery school with us. Nursery may have been no place for Lola long-term, but the children knew I lived with many happy animals and would welcome her into my family.

Lola, as she had just been named by my class, had a group of five-year-olds now fighting for her – an action group who, I realised as I watched them negotiate to save Lola, were always going to win. At first the carer was having none of our plans to save her. He found it funny and told them it was the circle of life.

'I'll be the one to teach them shapes,' I replied, and his worried face started to speak volumes.

A few temper tantrums and tears later, it seemed like a riot was about to break out. Eventually, he surrendered to the mounting pressure of Team Elementary. Lola was ours, and it was time to get her home. The sweet old lady seemed to understand the children wanted to and would help her. We made her a pretty collar from a bag handle and her lead was my belt.

Lola was happy to be walked out of hell by her knee-high saviours. On leaving the farm, the class loaded up onto the fifty-three-seater coach with moans and groans of 'we are taking Lola, aren't we?' and 'please don't leave her here'. My assurance excited them again. Tens of happy little faces stared out of the window to watch me load Lola. My little heroes had forgotten about their 3 o'clock biscuit and only had Lola on their minds.

Lola had pride of place on the backseat with me, safely buckled in. My talkative class greeted their parents with the news that Lola the sheep was on the coach – 'yes darling, I'm sure she is,' was the reply. Once the awaiting parents had collected their children, Lola and the rest of the class came into the school with me to await home time. Then into my latest rescue mobile (a Volkswagen Polo) Lola completed her final journey home to the safety of what would one day become The Retreat. In fact, she lasted longer than the Volkswagen Polo did.

CHAPTER EIGHT

EGYPT

One of my most memorable rescue stories from overseas was Suki the Egyptian goose. I had made Egypt my main overseas rescue project and I would base myself in Luxor helping the street and working animals. I met the most wonderful and supportive friends during my time there. They were the most supportive people and, despite being poor, never failed to welcome you into their homes and offer you a delightful meal. They would give you their last of anything. An incredible bunch of people who I loved spending time with. I adored Luxor with its history, ancient buildings, crazy drivers, dusty roads and street sellers. Just across the Nile from where I stayed was the Valley of the Kings and Queens, home to the famous Tomb of Tutankhamun, a place I loved to visit.

Each day I would set off to trap street cats and dogs and take them to the makeshift shelter for neutering. Most were so hungry it was an easy job. After the trapping I ventured onto the streets to check the carriage horses were doing okay: that they had water, good-fitting harnesses, no sores, good feet, teeth check, hay and shade when not working. Since the nights were cold, the horses also needed a rug thrown over them after sundown. I happily fetched and carried food, rugs and better-fitting tack for those horses I met. I would run to the animal hospital to get the vet when carriage drivers refused to help their sick and injured horses.

There was nothing I wouldn't do for the working horses, donkeys, mules and camels of Luxor. They worked so hard and received so little in return. Many of the regular animals I saw everyday recognised me and would know a treat and some kindness was coming their way. The positive changing attitude I saw towards working animals made all the hard work rewarding.

When I stopped for lunch, I would usually visit the animal markets and save as many as I could. I would buy and release pigeons and other wild birds, as well as rabbits and roosters, who I would set free in a field outside Luxor. A few times I got different types of waterfowl which I took down to the Nile and waved them off as they swam away from me down the river. It's a very satisfying feeling to see a newly released animal making its way to freedom.

The animal markets were soul-destroying, seas of cages piled high of the most terrified creatures. There was also rows of baskets full of puppies and kittens and larger animals tethered to market stalls. The only thing that kept me going were to save a soul and release them hoping for a brighter future. It wasn't unusual for my accommodation to be a nursing station between rescue and release. Hundreds of the most special souls touched my heart during this time, who's rescue I could tell the story of.

One such rescue came when I was back in the market, trying not to make eye contact with the many creatures needing help, when I knew deep down I could not save them all. I spotted what I thought was a sad, fat duck all alone. He was in the bottom basket and the droppings of the upper levels were falling through and covering him like the events with Dick the builder two-and-a-half-thousand miles away. The poor duck seemed like he'd given up and I could feel his sadness. I decided that he was the one rescue I had to make today – surely it would be easy to shoot down to the Nile to release him, then get straight back to work?

I paid the price to free the innocent death row prisoner who was waiting an unfair execution. The stall holder wrapped him in a small piece of string to secure his wings to hamper any escape plan he might have and handed over the terrified bird. My new rescue was so much larger than he first looked. More of a goose than a duck I smiled at him and kissed the top of his head. I named him Suki the Great. With him in my arms I could feel we had something special; the start of a unique friendship that would last the next ten years.

I cycled through the dusty streets of Luxor with my new friend tucked under my arm, looking like Rod Hull and emu doing the Tour de France. Most of the locals knew me and expected nothing less. I could feel Suki's heart banging with fear but I knew freedom would restore his happiness and that was just around the corner. Once I reached the steps of the Nile, I laid my bike down and set off for the great release. Suki seemed more and more excited to see the river.

'You're home now,' I whispered.

Some friends and locals had gathered to see what I was up to. I untied the string and Suki stretched his wings and was ready to go. I launched him on to the water and breathed a sigh of relief. To my absolute astonishment he sunk – was this the only goose in the world who could not swim? Suki unnaturally battled with the water, wings flapping and legs paddling ten to the penny for about a minute. By the time only his head and neck were visible above the water, I had realised I had to go in after him. Only taking one layer of clothing off I threw myself to the mercy of The Nile to save Suki the Great.

I landed and sunk like Suki had, and on coming up from the murky waters I could hear my friends calling what I though was 'Billy's-here'. I doggy paddled to try and catch the ailing goose to more cries of 'Billy's-here'. Suki was no match for my aquatic talents (doggy paddle Billy-style) I soon had him captured and back under my arm, we climbed ashore. I was soaked and worn out, holding a rather bemused goose who couldn't take his eyes off me.

It was only at this point my friends worriedly pointed out that they were not calling out in my honour of being a life-saving animal rescuer but more the name of the disease Bilharzia and not Billy's-here as I heard it. Bilharzia is a water-borne parasite, a disease that infects one in twelve Egyptians. Due to this horrid disease, every month a rural health official borrows the loudspeakers of the village mosques to summon those thought to be most at risk. They are then tested in an attempt to arrest the spread of the disease before it is too late. For me, this was just another trip to The Tropical Disease Hospital where they were starting to know me too. Thankfully I was one of those people who never got ill, no sore throat or common cold I'd usually manage to escape anything and once again I didn't catch the ugly ills of Bilharzia.

Back at the hotel, having cleaned Suki up and feeling

rather sorry for myself we settled down for a night in. It must be reported that right from the start Suki was a great house guest and enjoyed his pile of hotel towels to sleep on. He ate well enjoying most of the same foods as me including rice, vegetables, biscuits, corn and even falafel.

For the first few days I thought the staff of the hotel would not appreciate a goose gracing their premises, so I did my best for him to keep a low profile. If I left him alone, I would place the do-not-disturb sign on the door so Suki could rest without interruptions and I would learn to make the bed and clean the room. My hotel room had become a rehabilitation program to build Suki up for his next great release. Some hotel staff who I knew well would happily turn a blind eye about my unusual roommate but others may have not been happy.

Over the next few days I worked on getting Suki waterproof so he could take some swimming lessons. It wasn't long before my beautiful friend would follow me from our room on foot to the lift and take it to the rooftop pool at 5:30 every morning. Suki and I would have a swimming lesson for fifteen minutes with our instructor Mo, the hotel lifeguard. Mo had often promised me swimming lessons, but I always declined, since my workload meant I didn't have the time. Right now, I was so grateful for Mo's support. After our second lesson Mo decided that neither Suki nor I would ever be Olympic gold medallists for swimming. It was becoming more and more obvious that the only option for Suki's survival was to fly him back to the UK.

After getting the runaround for half a day I finally tracked down the local government vet and made an appointment to see him at his official residence. I set off on my bike again to start the wheels turning for Suki's departure from Egypt. The government vet was a larger than life character, an older official type with an air of eccentricity about him who insisted everything would be just fine. I felt he was an educated reliable person, a man who would help us. A man of his word?

A few crucial inoculations to prevent any duck diseases entering the UK and some simple paperwork all for a reasonable fee would be all we needed to rubber stamp our safe journey home. I left the rather empty dusty office thinking how easy it was to take a duck back to the UK – maybe lots of people did it? I excitedly cycled the streets of Luxor dropping off at friends to let everyone know that Suki would be flying home with me and what an absolute relief this was. I never gave it a second thought that the government vet wanted the procedure done at my hotel.

Four o'clock on the afternoon of the appointment I waited eagerly for the vet to arrive. I sat patiently outside the hotel chatting with the young children who were shoeshines and cleaners. These children had nothing but their happiness. I often thought just how hard it was for them just to survive, yet each one had a delightful smile. The difference between the children at home and these shoeshine kids, many younger than ten, was astonishing. I made a daily effort to look after each one of them and taught them all kindness like I did in my nursery school role. They were all so interested in the story of my goose that was going to fly to the UK when this was just a dream for them, a faraway place they may see on someone's TV.

As I waved to a carriage driver I had helped I heard the roar of an impressive motorcycle coming up the street, I looked up and watched with trepidation as it pulled over in front of me.

'Good afternoon, Mr Thompson,' the driver said, dressed in full motorcycle attire including a helmet. I realised it was the government vet who'd arrived on the back of a Harley Davison. Gobsmacked!

'Good afternoon,' I replied..

'Look after my bike and do not climb on her,' he barked at the children around us.

'They're good kids,' I replied, and he smiled condescendingly.

The vet followed me up in the lift that Suki and I had used to swim in the rooftop pool. This always brought a smile to my face, thinking *this goose doesn't need to fly, he can take the elevator*. My friend Mary, a short Cornish woman in her seventies, opened the door to let us in. Suki, with his usual picnic of fresh daily greens on a hotel towel sat in the middle of the room, head bobbing, tail wagging to welcome us. The vet got straight down to business and he told me the procedure was going to cost £200 in cash; of course I agreed, and he started to take off his jacket. A briefcase of paperwork and medical bits was laid out on the bed. Mary made us a coffee each and the vet drew up the injections. I wondered what both Suki and the vet thought at this stage, either that I was a mad English man or kind animal rescuer. I'm sure if Suki could have talked I would know the answer, but everyone was quiet at this stage.

The vet signed a few pages of official-looking documents and then elaborately crossing out large sections on the paperwork too, he then told me to sign in the boxes by his name. Maybe I should have looked closer to see if he'd signed on behalf of Tutankhamun, but I always think the best of everyone (it's kind of a birth defect). The small stickers from the vial were also placed on the documents too, making the whole episode seem authentic if not a little unconventional. He summoned me to hold the goose tight whilst he administered two injections, one against duck cholera and the other against Newcastle disease. The vet pushed the needle firmly into the feathers and I let out a cry.

'Please sir, Mr Thompson, this will not hurt the goose,' he said.

'No,' I cried, 'you've injected that into my hand!' The needle was deep inside my flesh. He had deposited the dose of duck cholera into my flesh – and didn't seem at all worried. He carried on with the Newcastle injection and then replaced the cholera jab. He assured me I would be fine, but my imagination ran wild. I started to think I'd wake up quacking and with feathers growing out of my ears, or worse, the symptoms of duck cholera. He thanked us for our business and on doing his jacket up he disappeared into the hallway and down to the street. He drove off on his newly polished Harley Davison – complements of the shoe shine kids – and with 200 quid in his back pocket for his services. Not bad for a half hour's work.

Later I started to worry that I might be coming down with duck cholera, and with Mary dancing to 'The Birdie Song' I decided to cycle to The Tropical Disease Hospital for the second time in ten days, where I was welcomed with a 'good afternoon Mr Thompson'. This place was quickly becoming my second home for all the wrong reasons. The duty doctor decided with a smile on her face that I would be fine, even if I now didn't need a plane to fly me home because I might just grow wings.

My friendship with Suki was growing every day. He settled down each night by my bed and shared the shower with me each morning, drying off in the sunshine that shone through the window. He seemed as happy as a dog would be when I came home and looked dejected when I was leaving.

Only a day before we would fly home I started to prepare for our travels. Usually I would give my clothes and shoes away to those who needed them most and any remaining money to the poorest families to help them and their working animals survive the hardships ahead. I would even leave without a suitcase on many occasions, literally travelling back to the UK with just the clothes on my back, wallet, passport and my favourite book of the trip. This time it would be different; I would travel home with my new friend, a memory of my work in Luxor I would never forget.

The airport was hot and busy. Everyone was incredibly interested that I was literally carrying a duck in a pet holdall. I checked in and asked where I should check Suki in. I was told I could carry my pet to the stairs of the plane where the aircraft staff would put Suki in the hold. I then went through passport control with more amusement and interest from travellers over my companion. I sat at my departure gate with Suki happily sitting on my lap, both of us eating crisps. Holidaymakers who were flying home on the same plane couldn't believe how I could just sit with my pet. The not-so-funny jokes from other passengers about 'what's on the menu' and 'orange sauce' grew more boring by the minute.

Eventually the flight was called for boarding and I took my place in the queue. 'Boarding pass' and 'have a safe journey' was all that was said, reassuring me that we would travel home soon. I took the stairs down to the plane – there was still no interest in Suki's paperwork. We took our place in a slow-moving queue across the tarmac and up the stairs of the Boeing. The families boarding the plane were thrilled to be part of this unique passenger's tale of adventure, but this was soon to come to an abrupt end. At the top of the stairs, I was stopped by an air hostess.

'Excuse me sir, what's that?' she asked me, her icy smile starting to defrost.

'Suki, my goose,' I replied.

'Well, I'm sorry but you can't bring that on here,' she said with a gobsmacked expression.

I pulled out Suki's paperwork, my secret weapon, and handed it over. The cabin crew closed ranks and turned their backs on me. I could hear them discussing the situation and unanimously deciding Suki could not come on the plane. I asked to speak to the pilot, to explain that the paperwork was all official and put together by the government vet.

'No, no, no,' was all the pilot said when he came out. 'Now put the goose down on the tarmac so you can board the plane and we can be on our way'. My blood starting to boil at being treated like a second-class citizen, I point-blank refused to do what I was told.

'What, just leave the bird on the tarmac? Over my dead body.' I made my way back down the stairs through the last of the awaiting passengers.

'That's right sir,' I could hear the air hostess saying condescendingly, 'just put the duck down and board the aircraft quickly.' I pointed out sternly that there was no way I would leave Suki. The air hostess made a last-ditch attempt at intimating me, telling me that backup was being called and that I'd be sorry if I ended up in prison. *In prison for what?* I thought. *Crimes against an airline with a lethal goose?* I waited patiently for them to change their mind whilst all other passengers boarded the plane home only two weeks before Christmas.

From across the tarmac I could see what looked like several army vehicles approaching me. Was this some sort of dream? Never one to feel threatened by uniforms or authorities, I promised Suki that we were in this together, and I wouldn't give up on her.

The army convoy stopped at the foot of the plane. The officers spilled out of the trucks with their machine guns just like something from a wartime blockbuster. They stood about awaiting orders and one senior officer came over to check out the mad English man and his feathered friend. On hearing it was not a drug smuggler or drunken passenger they smiled at me and nodded in support, to the disgust of the plane's crew who were determined to leave me behind now at any cost.

The pilot now demanded that I leave Suki and get on the aircraft, showing no consideration for the bird's welfare if left behind. He told me that missing our flight time would cost the airline a lot of money and that I could potentially be sued. It wasn't long until they realised no goose, no passenger: I was not shifting on this. On arranging a second flight time, they removed the stairs and taxied away onto a runway. The plane's windows were filled with many faces wondering what I would do, left on the tarmac with the light fading.

I looked at the bewildered ground crew for an indication of whether I could just leave. I was escorted back into the airport, just one man and his goose, and plonked myself down. I sat watching excited holiday makers and businessmen going on their way and I smiled to myself. What would I do? Where would we go? No cash or clothes, not even a toothbrush. I couldn't even get back to my hotel because I had no money for a taxi. Thankfully the only asset I had, everyone was interested in. I opened my book – *Songlines* by Bruce Chatwin – and hoping for some inspiration I sat in wait.

Babu, a vibrant, smartly dressed young travel rep I recognised from my hotel, was working the airport that night, greeting holidaymakers and making sure they found the right holiday transfer transport. Whilst directing new arrivals to their coaches he showed a fascination in my predicament and would occasionally smile and wave at me as he walked happy holidaymakers across the concourse. Curiosity finally won him over and he sidled across the polished floors to ask what was I doing in the airport with a goose.

The grin was soon knocked off his face when I gave him the short version of events. I asked if he knew how I could get back to Karnak with no money. Babu looked even more baffled.

'Back to Karnak with no money and a goose?' he replied. 'So you need a ride with a goose?'

'Yes!' I replied. I couldn't believe my luck when he said he finished at ten and could get me to Karnak. I only had to wait around for two hours and was eternally grateful for such kindness. I had only experienced love and kindness from the Egyptian people in all my endeavours. In the meantime, they proved themselves once more and Babu's work crew brought me water, falafel and salad which I'm sure was better than the in-flight meal served on the plane. To their amusements they even goose-sat Suki for me whilst I used the bathroom.

At ten everyone waved me good night and I walked with Babu to the parking lot. To my surprise, he didn't have a car but a moped. The bike had seen better days and I was sure it was missing a few parts, but it did have a seat. I rode on the back of Babu's bike with Suki wedged in between us; thankfully I had no luggage to grip hold of too. Whilst Babu zig-zagged in and out of the many obstacles on the tiny roads like, dogs, street sellers, carriage horses, large trucks, camels and free-roaming goats, I realised my life may never be normal. The sounds of horns, bells and sirens kept me focused even if I did have my eyes shut for most of the journey.

My entire life flashed before me serval times during my circuit of the Egyptian Grand Prix and I clung on for dear life. Luxor was especially beautiful at night with the many ruins and temples lit up; you could feel the magic and the ancient history. I could feel the pharaoh Queens Nefertiti, Hatshepsut and Cleopatra watching over us, their energy as strong today as if they still ruled Egypt.

We pulled up outside the hotel and I was thankful to be in one piece. Suki looked relaxed, not a single feather ruffed. After sizing up my chosen accommodation, Babu kindly offered to find me more reasonable digs. My original hotel suited Suki and me better because they knew us. Babu wanted more time to talk me through his business plans, the ones to make him a millionaire but I needed to go and negotiate with the hotel for a few night's accommodation without payment until my money would arrive.

Thankfully Cairo was on the desk and he looked puzzled when I walked back in. He was one of the sceptics who had found the government vet a little shady. I explained I needed my room back and I would settle up as soon as I got some money wired over. I also promised no more swimming lessons in the hotel pool for Suki. Cairo had known me for the three years I had been helping the animals of Luxor. I regularly brought him and his family gifts from the UK and we knew we could trust each other. Cairo asked me how I knew Babu who oddly enough was a distant cousin of his.

'We kind of met over a goose in the airport,' I replied.

My parents were always my most reliable road of help. My mum would always spring into action and come up with a plan to get me home safe. I also cleared it with Cairo that any calls to the UK would be added to my final hotel bill. I took a deep breath and called home. Mum was not even the slightest bit shocked at me missing another flight due to an animal needing my help. She had grown to understand that no matter what, animals would always come first, they had no one especially those animals in the meat markets.

'A goose refused entry to boarding the plane?' she said. 'How much do you need this time?' She told me that she would wire some money first thing in the morning via Western Union money transfer. I wondered what I would ever do without my parents. They were my get out of jail card, at least most of the time. There were times I was stranded penniless and hungry somewhere else in the world and I got Dad first on the phone I would tell my dad I hadn't eaten for three days and he would calmly reply, 'you really must force yourself,' followed by a deafening silence before his offers of help and a bout of laughter down the phone.

After speaking with my parents, I called around to rally the troops in support of Suki. One friend I called was the comedy writer Carla Lane, famous for writing hit TV sitcoms *The Liver Birds*, and *Butterflies* and *Bread*. Carla was an animal angel and she cared passionately about the plight of all creatures. We had met through animal rescue and our campaigning to end live animal exports at sea and airports across the country. Carla lived with hundreds of animals at her idyllic animal sanctuary, Animal Line in West Sussex.

In her soft and gentle voice Carla told me that of course she would help, and so she did. Carla did the ringing around DEFRA departments for hours finding out just how to get a duck legally from Egypt into the UK. She even offered Suki a home on one of her picturesque lakes when he was finally home safe.

It wasn't long until the press heard about Suki's story and my hotel room became an interview room, with newspapers and magazines calling up and running the story. Carla called in every day with an update and said we had even appeared on the news under duck rescue. On another occasion both Carla and her best friend Linda McCartney, also a great animal advocate, called me at the hotel to ensure me we would get Suki home. This would take time with so much red tape in acquiring one of the limited ornamental waterfowl import licences, but with Mum, Carla and Linda behind me I knew anything was possible.

The difficult part for me now was knowing I would need to fly home alone. The plan now was to find a goose sitter until Suki could come back. One of Babu's business ideas would now include a goose-sitting agency. Babu and I rode to the Western Union office to collect the money Mum wired over. Mum and Dad sorted a new ticket for me to fly home just days before Christmas and kindly offered to pay the hotel bill in full on my day of departure.

Over some falafel by the Nile I sold my idea to Babu, Egypt's equivalent to Alan Sugar. Babu was desperate to start a leisure boat business on the Nile but had no set-up funds, and he also wanted to visit the UK. I listened to numerous other business ideas and travel plans and I could feel his hunger to make it in life. I offered him help with the leisure boat idea and invited him to stay with me and my family in the UK. We sealed the deal with another coffee.

That night I reported back to each caller that Suki would be in the safe hands of Babu's Goose Sitter Agency and that, as and when the legitimate licences came through, Babu would send him on his way. Back in the UK, Suki the superstar appeared on the news again titled *Duck Rescue Update*; he took it all in his stride and, settling down for the evening he ate a little more corn.

I had all the trust in the world in Babu to help make this fairy-tale rescue come true. He was an honest and trustworthy friend and during my short time with him, I joined his family like a brother and a son. Babu and I worked hard to build a house and run at his home for Suki. I felt heartbroken at leaving him but knew the time had come for me to return and make his journey to the UK as smooth as possible. Suki looked happy and settled in his new abode and I said my goodbyes full of tears. My ride to the airport on the back of the moped flew by and before I disappeared into the airport I hugged Babu and thanked him for all he had done, knowing that Suki was in safe hands.

The plane journey home was emotional, so I decided to sleep the whole flight. I could think about nothing but Suki. It actually took a further seven months of red tape and a couple of stopovers in other countries to get him home. First, Suki flew to Cyprus to a friend of a friends and then to a contact in France three months later. From France, we managed to get the ornamental waterfowl import licence sorted. The last leg of Suki's journey was by van and the day he arrived at Carla's sanctuary we had a welcome party waiting for him. We had all his favourite foods laid out and there was a party of other ducks and geese waiting for him to come out of his box. Suki was now safe in paradise, home at last with everything he needed. This may have been one of my longest rescues, but the moral of the story is to never give up, for every animal deserves that chance.

CHAPTER NINE

A UNION

During my twenties I loved and lost. I juggled relationships with my 24/7 rescue world, campaigning and a few career moves, trying to find that one thing that ignited my passion like animals did. I had jobs where I would set up hospital areas for pigeons in storage cupboards out of sight of my boss and use the bottom filling cabinet draw to conceal a litter of hand-rearing piglets that needed feeding every twenty minutes. My desk draw was converted for tiny naked rodent babies sleeping on a hot water bottle. If there was no space to help animals in the office, my car parked outside would have boxes with hand-rearers inside, creatures on medication and others who needed regular build-up feeds.

Between work, my animals and relationships I attended demos to highlight the plight of the animals. I picketed wild animal circuses, animal testing centres, ban live export rallies and other activities up and down the country. Those diverse years taught me so much. I also met some of my dearest friends like Anabel and Rob Roach (whose four special children, Billy, Chloe, Amber and Daisy, I am godfather to), Diane and Dave Hogg whom we still city-break around the world with every year, and their two daughters (another two of my god daughters), Indy and Autumn. Other heroes and great friends I made at this time include Kate Owns

(Mozzie), Yvonne Perkins, Matt and Lara, Danuta, Soraya, Greta and Paul. Ros and Gerald, Jane, Lynda, Myrna and Simon, Joan, Val and her mum Pam and daughters Jodie and Ellie from our weekly vigils at the Dover docks campaigning to end the vile trade in the exports of live animals.

These friends are so selfless in their actions to make positives changes in our world, and they changed my life forever. Each one of them is carved into my heart. Together we had great breakthroughs in helping end many terrible cruelties to so many animals. We celebrated stopping live exports from many seaports as well as Coventry airport where very young calves were flown to destinations to end their lives in veal crates.

Sadly, at this time an incredible young woman campaigner called Jill Phipps was killed when a live export lorry drove over her. Jill came from a committed family of campaigners who were left devastated and with no justice due to the murderer never being charged. Jill's funeral was held in Coventry Cathedral to a full house of ordinary people who not only sympathised with the cause but the loss of a young mother too. The campaign to end live export brought about a great deal of media activity and even the screen legend Brigitte Bardo, a renowned animal campaigner, flew in to attended Jill's funeral and pay her respects.

Other victories came from closing down Windsor Safari Park and its cruel Orca tank, Hillgrove Farm, the last UK breeder of cats for medical research, Consort, breeders of beagles for animal testing, Shamrock farm, traders in monkeys for medical research, and Regal Rabbits and New-church Guinea Pigs, both supplying laboratories for cruel and unnecessary animal testing. Wild animal circuses were outlawed too. It seemed like nothing could stop us. The list of anti-animal practises we stopped goes on and is a show of people's power and dedication to right over wrong. My flat was now not only a rescue centre for animals but many human characters I brought home and looked after. Many became great friends who I'm still friends with today, and we became a great network of rescuers.

One rainy December evening I attended the annual Trafalgar Square Christmas tree presentation, a gift every year from the Norwegian prime minister. The Norwegian government was still killing whales against the International Whaling Commission's strict protocol, so a protest was called. Protesters filled the square and mingled with the festive well-wishers. A cheerful choir sang carols, and everyone gleefully sang along. The atmosphere was so joyful and Christmassy, then the prime minister took to the stage. The clapping of cold hands stopped (unlike the rain) and just as he started his speech, I shouted above the volume of his microphone: 'NORWAY STOP THE BLOODY WHALING'. A very disappointed Norwegian prime minister stopped and stared at me, embarrassed, as the police removed me from the crowds and escorted me out of the square to the steps of the National Gallery. I heard the prime minister start again only for another protester to drown him out. I was warned not to return down the stairs to the event or I would be arrested, and the police hurried off to remove the next protestor.

The rain had started to fall heavier and with no umbrella I wondered if I should just go home. I turned to face the South African Embassy in the direction of Charing Cross station and was confronted by a tall older woman maybe in her mid-sixties wearing a raincoat with the collar up and a black beret. She was smoking a cigarette from some sort of holder and I also noticed she was wearing odd espadrilles (one red and one blue) in the pouring rain. She looked like something from the French Resistance in the TV show *Hello Hello* and I half expected her to say with a French accent, 'I will say this only once'. Instead she praised me on my loud bellowing message to the prime minister. *What a character,* I thought. She asked if I wanted to eat something and before I could answer she pointed the way.

We wandered off to the back streets off Covent Garden and arrived at a restaurant called Jimmy's, and I followed her in. She seemed to know her way around, so I carried on behind her and down the stairs. Here, my new friend was met with resistance and ordered to leave by the restaurant manager. Surprisingly, she kept her cool – more than I would have done in the circumstances. She calmly leant into him and had a private word in his ear. He looked me up and down and with gritted teeth led the way through the restaurant. All then seemed well and we were seated.

The restaurant had a long, fitted-bench against one wall, running down the inside of the whole building, with small tables, and opposite chairs placed along it. It created a nice space for couples to have a romantic meal in the dim light, maybe somewhere I would even visit again. Each table had a wine bottle encased in a basket with a burning candle in the top. I understood why Claudine had chosen this restaurant; it really had something even after the frosty reception to start with. Claudine acknowledged the couple sitting next to us and with real grace squeezed onto the bench. I took the chair opposite her. For the older couple seated next to us the arrangement was reversed. They were so deeply into each other they barely noticed us.

Claudine told me that she had climbed the ranks of the Royal Ballet. Her well-spoken voice, good skin and Notting Hill address would have led anyone to believe she was rich and famous or at least married into aristocracy, even if her shoes said otherwise. Instead, she went on to tell me that she was broke and always had been. Her flat a few levels up belonged to a social housing trust where she had hoarded her two true loves, art and cats, for years. She explained this to me in between ordering wine, green olives and her favourite pasta dish to share. She winked at the waiter and offered him a cigarette. She seemed to know the whole team, but I could feel the hostility towards her. I wondered to myself why she kept coming here when the staff seemed so resentful towards her – surely the pasta was not that good.

Just as I started to ask if she visited Jimmy's a lot, Claudine picked up her fork and, to my shock, leaned across to the other couple's table. She twisted their spaghetti onto her fork and proceeded to eat a heap of their food. I sat frozen to the chair my heart beating through my chest.

'Claudine, what do you think you're doing?' I snapped at her.

'I won't tell if you won't,' she said without a moment's hesitation. I turned to the shocked couple, who wanted nothing more than to be left alone, and apologised profusely on behalf of my dinner guest.

Was Claudine completely mad? Yes, I decided. Who does

such a thing? Like a scene from a silent movie she mimed to me that he was wearing a wedding band and the woman he was with was not. Holy macaroni, I thought, what was I doing? It was at this point I realised I also had no wallet; I thought I would just get up pay and leave, but all I had in my pockets were my door key, return train ticket home and approximately £2.

Since Claudine had invited me to eat, she could surely make the payment. She continued to talk to me through the highs and lows of her life, ballet school, her top performances, failed marriages and how she escaped a violent husband in Turkey with her cats. Recently she had suffered a bereavement when her boyfriend threw himself from her art studio window and was impaled on the iron railings below.

'I'd never been able to open that window,' she told me with a puzzled look on her face and no show of sadness for her dead lover. Apparently, she was now dating a penniless Earl by the name of Shackleton who did low-cost funerals from the back of his Land Rover, which right now was clamped she explained. With the wave of a hand she ordered another bottle of wine. I felt for sure now that I should approach the subject of the bill. The second bottle of wine arrived and she washed it down, cool as a cucumber.

The couple next to us who had had their private rendezvous exposed stood up to leave. Claudine knowingly nodded at the woman and winked at the man. The disgusted couple left. I finished my half glass of remaining wine for Dutch courage.

'Thanks for a lovely evening,' I said, 'but I've got to catch my train.' Claudine nodded.

'Just sort the bill on your way out, because I'm hanging about,' she replied. My stomach sank.

'Claudine, I'm so sorry but I didn't bring anything because I was on the protest,' I told her.

A look of disappointment came over her face and explained she had whispered to the restaurant manager that I was taking her to dinner when she was refused entry earlier.

'Well you're surely not expecting me to foot the bill, I can't afford all that – I told you I was penniless.'

'I would never have ordered the wine, the pasta, the olives if I had come alone,' she replied, not looking the slightest bit embarrassed.

The original member of the team who had not wanted to let Claudine in approached me and asked what if there was a problem. I explained to him in detail and he asked disapprovingly if it was normal for me to promise older ladies a meal and then not be able to afford such luxuries.

'Hardly – I'm gay,' I replied to his ludicrous suggestion. 'This isn't something I normally do, it's just a misunderstanding.'

'Well, it's a misunderstanding that needs to be paid for right now,' the restaurant manager said.

Claudine, sitting back enjoying the entertainment and the last of the wine, seemed more than comfortable in this situation. I asked if I could use the restaurant's phone to call my boyfriend to sort out this awkward mess. I couldn't believe my ears when in the background I heard Claudine order a limoncello on my bill. I finally got my boyfriend on the phone who was relived I was not ringing from the police station to say I'd been arrested at the anti-whaling protest and happily provided the restaurant manager the details of his American Express card to sort out the misunderstanding.

Oddly enough, my alliance with Claudine continued after this, but we never went for dinner again. Claudine became my go-to person for picking up injured Central London pigeons and she would happily take the train to deliver the birds to me. I look back at that shocking meal as a business meeting for the birds of London.

I continued to meet the most incredible characters, young and old, male and female under the cover of darkness helping the neglected and stray animals of London and Kent, doing everything they could with what they had. I wrote poems about the most eccentric of them and each of the other ones gained a nickname with links to where I met them or what they had dedicated their life to saving. Poems like, '*Mike Costello a rather odd fellow, it's not that's he's strange or even deranged, He's just Mike Costello, a rather odd fellow*', about a great pigeon rescuer called Mike Costello. We still give people nicknames today – names like Julie Cob, PJ pigeon June, Multi-Cat Clair, K9 Keith, Renee Mead-Feral Feed, Viv the Vixen, Tow-bar Sue, Wonder Woman, Welsh Bob, Chatty Patty, Betty Spaghetti, Brid-Beans, Squirrel-Mummies Sally and Pam, Combat-Val, GPS Guinea Pig Scott, Skippy (Greta), Mozzie Kate, Shiver, Nanny Moo Moo, Miss Mina, Dogbite and Superdog are all awarded to our saintly animal people in honour of their tireless work.

Jannette Fergus AKA Wonder Woman was aptly named after being the only person to get into The Retreat during a four-day snow blizzard. Jannette, never one to take no for an answer drove her ageing Ford Mondeo with shovel in the boot the eight or so miles to help the residents of The Retreat. A true Mrs Doubtfire, born in Glasgow and made of girders, a southern blizzard was nothing to her. So, through the snowdrifts, heavy snowfall and icy roads she drove the dangerous tracks of Kent to get to her beloved residents. A few times on route when many other travellers had abandoned their cars and journeys, she dug herself out and continued with her drive. To our amazement she drove off the bright white lane that not even 4x4s were getting up and started to unpack her food parcels for the animals. She was nicknamed Wonder Woman from that day on and she still brings us food parcels every week whatever the weather.

Tow-bar Sue gained her nickname from being our only contact at the time with a tow-bar. Her Land Rover helped us out and we never forgot it. She was awarded her nickname which we still use today and even many years without a tow-bar she's still called TBS. TBS is also one of our outstanding homes for those dogs who need someone special to live with. These are two of the unsung heroes of The Retreat that are instrumental in our success.

One Saturday during the winter of 1995, whilst on a fur protest in central London I met a warm and kind woman called Gloria. She seemed to radiate an inner glow – and shared my sense of humour – and immediately I knew we would be friends for life. When we met, Gloria was fifty-two and I was twenty-five.

Gloria would go on and introduce me to the love of my life, human that is. She was a divorcee and lived with her twenty-three-year-old gay son, one dog and twelve cats in an old Victorian converted house in Tulse Hill, London. Gloria knew how to have a good time and her flat became a second home to me.

Jamie, Gloria's son, was a talented DJ in the gay clubs of London and a great chef. Jamie was also very kind and gentle, and adored his animal family too. Animals had brought us all together and cemented a friendship that's still alive today. Little did I know that in less than a year I would have leaped from one relationship to another, only this one was forever, thanks to Gloria.

One warm long summer's evening Gloria had a get-together at her flat. It's had been a scorching day and an evening of socialising seemed just the thing to finish off a great day. Gloria had the Victorian sash windows wide open to catch any breeze and I could hear Jamie's music playing from the streets below. Gloria and Jamie's friends filled the flat and the usual atmosphere was relaxed and friendly.

Jamie's friend Aly and her brother Neil had come along for the soirée. Both were living in Shepherd's Bush but originally from the Welsh Valleys just outside Bridgend. I noticed Neil and immediately checked him out, and when he smiled back my heart missed a beat. He had the most gorgeous thick long blond hair and shinning blue eyes. No one had ever caught my eye like he did that epic summer's evening. He was wearing a fitted white shirt and faded jeans rolled up; no socks and his second-hand boat shoes. He looked iconic but we didn't get to chat – we weren't even introduced to each other. I left that evening and couldn't stop thinking about him on the drive home.

It was a few weeks later that Gloria mentioned to me that Aly and Neil lived in a flat share where the cats needed neutering and a few litters of kittens needed good homes. I was given the job to go to West London and help sort out the growing problem of Neil's landlady's multi-cat issues. I drove over in my latest animal rescue vehicle filled with cat boxes, blankets and cat food. I arrived late and parked alongside the large detached house that was split into flats. The leafy road in Shepherd's Bush seemed impressively quiet for being located between Goldhawk and the Uxbridge Road. I was ready to solve any of the feline families' problems. The cats were well loved and looked after; they just needed a practical idea for birth control. All the flat sharers and more were there ready to give advice and offer a helping hand.

I boxed up the little fluffy families and assured everyone the mums and one baby each would be home tomorrow after their operations and MOT. The other kittens would be happily adopted by people wanting to give a forever home to pairs of the babies. Kittens and puppies, like all baby animals, would always be the easiest to find homes for. Altogether, there were seven adults and approximately twenty kittens. Each little mum got the once-over by the vet and was microchipped before their neutering operation. I returned a few mums with a kitten each to their happy home and my reward was a cup of tea with Neil. The more time I spent with him, the more I liked him – and he really cared about animals too. Neil played it cool, giving nothing away about his feelings for me. I had one last look at the sleeping mums and kissed the kittens goodbye.

I set off to do a few pick-ups of wildlife from vets on my way home, to add to those recovering at home. With my car full of pet carriers empty and full I made my way home but could only think of Neil.

My last chance to see Neil came the following Saturday night. Gloria was leaving London for Banbury, Oxford, where she and Jamie would continue to help stray and unwanted animals, and was holding a party to say goodbye to everyone. Gloria's party marked the end of an era. I spent most of the evening chatting with Neil and watching him throw back his blonde locks and chat about what life ahead held for him. I couldn't think how I would ask him out during our deep conversations. He was so kind and gentle and had an authentic feel about him which I'd struggled to find in someone since Joe had passed.

In true Gloria and Jamie style, everyone had a great evening, even if it was overshadowed by the fact that the hostess with the mostess would be leaving us. The guests started to say their long emotional goodbyes and were slowly leaving but Neil and I sat oblivious in deep conversation. I finally found the courage to ask him if he wanted a lift home; I couldn't miss my opportunity even if he did live the other side of London. To my surprise, he said yes! Gloria's Cupid bow and arrow had worked and I'm sure it was always her plan.

On leaving the party my phone was ringing with calls of help for injured wildlife and a stray cat in New Cross. The normally tedious journey to Shepherd's Bush was a blend of laughter and serious life plans. The more Neil spoke, the more I liked him, from his delicate lips to his long fingers, I couldn't find fault. He talked about his family: his mum, Margaret, back in Wales, his gay sister, Aly, who flat shared with him (who I'd already met), his three brothers, Peter,

Alan (married to Debbie) and Lyn (married to Clare), all back home in Wales. Neil also mentioned his other sister, Maggie, who lived in Canada with her husband Paul and two children. Neil's dad, Roy, had been a miner and a great family man, and had passed away a few years ago. Neil told me they had been very similar.

Neil had a large family who he was very proud of, and in this way he reminded me of myself and how I felt for my own family. We were very clearly made for each other, but I couldn't get a word in edgeways. It didn't occur to me that this life story was more about Neil's nervousness in anticipation of working up the courage to proclaim his feelings for me. We were both trying to find the courage to say how we felt.

Eventually I pulled over and parked outside Neil's flat. I turned off the engine and immediately an awkward deafening silence fell upon us. We sat in the dark for what felt like eternity and I would notice Neil's every move, even the blink of his eye. I was just about to come out with something corny like, '*Do you want to go out sometime soon for a drink*' when Neil turned to me.

'Billy,' he said softly, 'what would you say if I told you I had feelings for you?' I couldn't believe it.

'What took you so long?' I replied. We laughed, and with a fairy-tale kiss, Neil said goodnight and climbed out of the car.

The very next day I drove back to Shepherd's Bush after a sleepless night, this time not for the cats but to pick Neil up and take him on a very special date. Today he was going to meet my collection of horses, goats and sheep living in the fields outside of London. Neil had packed a picnic and en route home we would stop at The Loft to meet the rest of my animal family.

The day at the fields was magical. We laid out the picnic blanket on the long grass, surrounded by relaxed horses, goats and sheep spending the day with us. The fields were tucked away from the hassle of everyday life; they were their own bubble of kindness and freedom for the few creatures that had made it out of a world that commodifies animals only for profit.

That afternoon stretched into one of those long hot September days and with the sun on our faces we fell asleep to the sound of snoring horses and sheep trying to eat the last of the picnic. This perfect afternoon was to become a landmark in our relationship where for years after we would always try to picnic on 14th September with our animal family. Thankfully, Neil was a natural with the animals – everyone just loved him. From naughty dogs to wild cats they all found Neil's calm and gentle presence a beacon of love, just like I did.

That night, Neil stayed at the flat and we talked into the early hours about ways we could help more and more animals. In true gentlemanly style, I made Neil a bed up in the lounge and he was most likely thinking he would fall asleep to the soft sounds of purring for the array of old cats around the lounge. Instead it was the harrowing sounds of Hank and Storm, my irritable-bowel cats scratching their litter boxes and making the most horrendous attempts at depositing something ghastly in honour of our new guest.

Each day for the next two weeks we both sent each other a

letter, card or notelet. We also tried to touch base daily over the phone, and the hours would just run away. The following weekend, excited to see Neil again in the flesh, I was of course late for our date in Leicester Square. We were going to eat somewhere and then go to the cinema to see a horror called *The Last Supper*. I had been out trapping feral cats just up the road in Battersea and I desperately wanted to catch the last skinny mum, having caught all the others. I could tell that the car from where I was trapping stank of tomcat, or maybe I did, but I didn't care; I was in love. With the close of the trap door on skinny Minnie I filled the car with the many newly rescued cats and made a quick dash across Albert Bridge, up through Belgravia, around Hyde Park Corner with a royal wave and down to Chinatown.

With the cats comfortable in their baskets with beds and biscuits, I parked on a double yellow line and ran down to the square. *Who cares if I'm clamped? Neil's worth it*, I thought. There I found Neil, very smartly dressed and having waited patiently for me despite the rain. He explained that we would have to miss dinner due to my lateness, and go straight for the film. *The shape of things to come*, I thought to myself, with so many missed dinners, get-togethers, parties, flights and trains because somewhere an animal needed us.

It was this very night that we talked about Neil moving in the following weekend, just two weeks since we had expressed how we felt for each other. Our union was one of knowing *this is it*, right from the start. A life of togetherness, helping others, sometimes even before ourselves. There was no doubt Neil clearly knew what he was letting himself in for and was looking forward to making a difference to the lives of thousands of animals who had no one to help them. He was ready to be part of the unofficial 24/7 rescue team that served London, Kent, and elsewhere.

Once Neil moved in, the rescue work got easier and so did managing the menagerie at home. It didn't take long until we were moving closer to our family in the fields of Kent. Everyone was coming along, from Mighty the sparrow to Eden and Ava the lurchers. Pigeons, rats and cats would all be relocated to the tiny house we were moving to – and tiny was an understatement. The house known as Mouse Hall would now be our home for the next few years.

The front door opened into one room which was our living space and a small kitchen tucked away under the stairs, and a bed space and bathroom upstairs. We added a bespoke mahogany conservatory which doubled our living space. It also housed the plants, large and small birds like Bev the broiler chicken, Gomez the turkey and Mighty, as well as Parsnip the lamb and a selection of the dogs. The lounge was home to rabbits, rats, chinchillas and most of the dogs. The tiny kitchen was gated which worked for bottle feeding babies like Leo the foal, Grace and Ellie goat kids and many others. Most of the old cats and very old dogs slept upstairs, and the bathroom doubled as a kind of pre-release site for wild birds. When we had a water or sea bird in, the bath would be adapted to shallow pond with rocks etc thankfully we would bath at my sisters just around the corner.

The postage-stamp garden was swallowed up by conservatory, but we made real use of the remaining space. Neil created a beautiful Chinese border around the outside of the new building with bamboo and stone water features which added the only sense of peace in our new tiny home. We discovered we had an outstanding neighbour who had come from three generations of vegetarians.

Jeneen and Peter lived in the expensive townhouses just across the way with one tiny, beautiful daughter, Morgan, and lots of animals. Jeneen's mum Gisela, who visited daily, was a picture of health and glamour and was our go-to vegetarian for showing people what a difference a plant-based diet had on our older generations. Jeneen very kindly donated me many of Peter's good clothes which I happily wore to work. They would also babysit any creature I dropped off and on one occasion, when knocking on the door to give Jeneen my latest baby, Peter answered. Looking me up and down he asked, smiling, if I'd like a pair of his shoes to go with his trousers and top I was wearing.

'No no no,' I replied, 'but could you please babysit Maisie, the week-old piglet whilst I show my face at work?'

I was absolutely blessed to have such support right from the start from them, and now they are my dearest of friends. Another great neighbour-come-friend was Ronnie and his dog, Scrappy, who walked past twice a day on his way to feed the foxes and birds in the park. It made my day if I got to chat with old Ron and Scrappy.

Neil was now about three years into the rescue world and had taken to it quite well. He had decided there should be a limit to the number of animals we brought into the house. He continued to discuss his almost business strategy to stem the surge of intakes. Looking around the house he decided that dogs, cats and rabbits had reached capacity and we must learn to say no, *let there be no more emotional blackmail when it comes to animals needing our help*, he told me. A firm line should be drawn when faced with needy animals and their pushy owners. *Easier said than done,* I thought, but I'd let our very own Che Guevara find his own way. Eventually, I agreed that Neil should be in charge of intakes – from now on he would say no and turn his back on some animals, refusing to be blackmailed into going over our agreed capacity for residents.

The very next morning over breakfast, Neil reiterated his very own No Policy with remarks like 'Am I clear? No more dogs.' He then left home on the first of the three buses he took to work.

My own transport to work was our newly acquired wheelchair-friendly van, which looked like a less loved version of the famous Popemobile and was no longer required by the family after their disabled relative had died. The back doors opened and there was a ramp for a wheelchair to fit in, and there was a row of seats before the driver and passenger seats. The vehicle was ideal for us and with dogs seated in each window, our neighbours soon christened her 'The Poochmobile'. With her high roof over the back and windows all round, a person could remain comfortably in their wheelchair and see out. She had one fault and that was the fuel gauge never worked, but for a free animal ambulance it was a small price to pay.

That evening, to my absolute surprise, Neil AKA Che Guevara returned home and, coming through the front door with a trembling female greyhound on the end of his belt.

'You won't believe it,' he said. The poor starving girl was terrified of just about everything. She climbed onto the sofa and hide her face in the cushions. I quizzed Neil about his No Policy and *'Am I clear? No more dogs'.*

'How could I turn my back on her and just leave her when she ran onto the bus behind me shaking with fear because of the thunder and lightning?' Neil said.

'Calm down,' I said, 'she's safe with us now.' She just wanted someone to make it ok for her, cover her eyes and hold her tight.

'She needs food and warmth somewhere safe and I couldn't see her turned off the bus,' Neil said. 'I claimed her to the people of the bus.'

It was a baptism of fire and Che Guevara had to face his own revolution. This was what I was faced with every day, and the moral of the story was not to say no, just to find that little extra space to squeeze one more in. After all, it was just one more dog bed…

The night after Grace the greyhound arrived, I received a rescue callout. The caller had spotted a large injured bird in a village outside of Bromley. I set off in The Poochmobile – containing everything you need for rescue work and more – on tonight's rescue job. When I finally arrived in the right country lane after numerous false alarms, I couldn't believe my eyes.

I was confronted with a juvenile ostrich, about six feet tall and very distressed, with an injured leg. Where had he come from? Were there others? I was alone on the rescue and even though he was injured he could run and put up a fight. After being outrun a few times and a few battles with his wings, I decided to push him into a gateway where I could use The Poochmobile to block him in. The stressful circumstances made him less obliging to my help and then he took to using his legs as his other defence. After a struggle of about three hours I decided the only way forward was to rugby tackle him and wrap him up in the dog blankets.

Obviously, I didn't have a cage in the The Poochmobile big enough for an ostrich. My new friend fought through the blanket and could pack a punch with his head, leg or wing. Eventually he lost the fight and a bound and gagged ostrich was coming home with me. With both back doors open I pushed and pulled the prehistoric creature onto the ramp, reassuring him there was plenty of room at home for a bird who could live for seventy-five years. Up the ramp he went and with a slight head tilt and leaning himself onto the back seats I shut both the doors. I leant back onto the doors and wondered what on earth Neil would say. As I carefully drove home around the winding lanes the dreaded thought of the fuel gauge and alarm bells at how many miles I had done started to worry me. I couldn't use a fuel station but what if I broke down? My rescuer would find me and an ostrich standing in the wheelchair area of The Poochmobile.

Thankfully, I made it home and explained to Neil about the new arrival in The Poochmobile. We both had smiles on our faces and maybe Neil a little disbelief in his heart. He wondered out loud if perhaps the bird was a big heron, pelican or turkey, then followed me out to help lead the bird into the house.

'He's an ostrich,' Neil said with disbelief. Our ostrich was all covered up like he was someone famous avoiding the paparazzi and into the house he went.

Once he was in the kitchen, we could asses the damage

done to his leg. A further fight kicked off in the small space which resulted in Neil's newly cooked spaghetti being thrown around the place. *No dinner tonight then?* Thankfully the damage to the ostrich's leg was superficial – just a few cuts and grazes and nothing a good clean up couldn't solve. Now all we needed to do was find the ostrich a good home and get him out of our kitchen.

Later that night, with a blanket over the kitchen window and one across the kitchen opening, Hector The Ostrich started to settle down and I even saw him pick at the spaghetti he'd thrown around earlier; maybe he thought it was an anaemic worm? It didn't prove an easy adoption trying to find someone who knew what they were doing with ostriches, so a few nights at the best animal bed and breakfast in Kent was Hector's only option. After all, the restricted area of the tiny kitchen was good for his injured leg. Whilst everyone in our rescue circle worked hard to find an ostrich-friendly home we ate chips for dinner, unable to use the kitchen.

Five days into our Hector Boy living in the kitchen and happily drinking from the kitchen sink and Neil complaining he was pecking his plums in the fruit bowl, there was a loud official knock at the door. Several of the dogs began growling, and I knew it would be a stranger. I opened the front door a fraction to an official-looking man with a clipboard standing on the doorstep. He informed me that he was from TV licensing, and asked why I didn't have a TV license. What a waste of human resources, I thought, to send someone to call at the homes of people with no TV.

'Surely you need a TV to have a license?' I replied, with the dogs snapping at my heels.

'Yes,' he replied, and told me that he had been watching us watch TV through the small window near my front door.

'That's actually my neighbour's window, not mine,' I replied, thinking this would be the end to the interrogation. I couldn't be the only person in the UK with no TV – why have one when I had no time to watch one? Instead, the irritated caller insisted on coming in to check that there was no TV on the premises.

My usual operation to remove the canine bodyguards probably sounded like me stashing a TV behind the sofa, but this was the norm in our house. I reopened the door and invited the man in with a fake smile on my face. Once aboard Noah's Ark, he cast his eyes around in disbelief at the wall that divided us from our neighbour's TV. This was no normal house; our Ark was stacked with piles of cages of rodents awaiting their forever homes, was dog bed central and also contained a forest of unwanted plants through the glass door, along with a zillion snarling faces.

'No TV out there either,' I pointed out.

'What about upstairs?' he said.

'After you,' I said in my most condescending voice. He peeked quickly into the bedroom at our collection of sweet old cats snoring away; nothing would wake them apart from the tap of a tin. His eyebrow lifted when he pushed open the bathroom door to find a waterpark of a half-filled bath, rocks with real swimming gulls and Spartacus, our hand-reared gull, standing on the back of the toilet.

'Satisfied?' I barked at him, and we went back down the stairs.

'What's in there?' the caller asked, pointing to the hanging blanket. I wondered if he'd believe the truth if I told him there was an ostrich in my kitchen.

'It's the kitchen,' I said firmly, 'and there's no TV in there.'

'Would you mind if I took a look for myself?' said the caller.

'I really don't think it's a good idea,' I replied.

Without my permission the caller pulled back the blanket to the darkened space and as he leaned over in search of the absent TV I heard a lethal thump of Hector's foot and immediately his 'right hook' of wing crashing into the centre of the caller's face. Due to the darkness I don't think he could make out quite what had just happened, but without a doubt he knew not to lean back in.

His face said it all and I thought of a million funny lines to use, like *he's just a budgie on steroids,* or, *hasn't he outgrown the kitchen,* or even, *they said he was a Minor bird when I bought him.* I escorted him to the front door and noticed his lip was bleeding. Without so much as a goodbye, he disappeared up the road to his van, never looking back. A few days later Hector was offered a fantastic home with other ostriches up county, and Neil and I happily took him there in The Poochmobile. The following night we returned home, and Neil could once again cook a spaghetti without fighting for space with an ostrich.

CHAPTER TEN

FROM TINY ACORNS

Our tiny home was a happy one, and it served us and our family well. It was the hub of the South of England rescue response team (namely me). There were no red tape or telephone operators to put you in touch with a nine-to-fiver who was just about to go off shift and couldn't help; if I got the call I went out to help the animal, no 'sorry, it's my day off'.

There was still so much to learn and thankfully I had great friends who had been helping animals far longer than I had, including Paula and Ernie who started Hopefield Animal Sanctuary in Brentwood, Essex, and would always give me sound advice. My friend and illustrator Danuta Mayer was also an amazing source of knowledge and support. Danuta had once given me a beautiful book she had illustrated called *Tenzin's Deer*. The book by Barbara Soros was about a young boy who finds an injured deer and aids his recovery. The book goes on with the lesson of learning to know when to let go. It was a great story of strength which helped me release the many wild animals I nursed back to good health.

One such deer was Roscoe, a young buck found caught on a fence and starving hungry. During the rearing of wild animals, it's very important to keep them as wild as possible. It's not the easiest of practices because most of us rescuers want to love and nurture everything, but we all must do our best to get those creatures back out into the wild where they belong. The wilderness runs in their blood and being fully alive is to be free.

Roscoe had his way of telling me when he was ready for his bottle: he would call out like a calf or a lamb. I fed him without the interaction I give to our calves and lambs so he could one day be released and find a family of his own. When his time came, I took him along to a safe and deer-friendly estate where he would find others of his kind. I manoeuvred the deer box into a position for the release, the young buck ready and eager to go. His instinct was strong, and his time had come. It was at this point I thought about all the horrors that face our beautiful wildlife and questioned whether this was right for Roscoe.

I remembered the moral of *Tenzin's Deer*, that kind gift from Danuta and a few words came to mind: 'may no harm come to you'. I knew what I had to do, just as Tenzin did, and I emotionally opened the box and set him free. He wandered down the track and disappeared behind an old oak tree. My heart sank, wondering what he would eat, and whether he would meet a friend. Roscoe stopped and looked at me – it really penetrated deep into my soul – and with a call that was usually for his bottle he took off into the woodland. That heartfelt moment reminded me of what the power of kindness can achieve.

Another milestone in the foundations of our incredible story was when my parents purchased some land in Crockenhill to ease the pressure of our growing family. The land had some amazing neighbours, most of whom were great animal lovers. One neighbour, Pamela (Pam) Webster and her husband Ian were very helpful in keeping an eye out whilst I wasn't there. Both Pam and Ian were dedicated in helping me help animals. They were newly married and had just moved to their bungalow by the fields. They were born entertainers too and loved nothing better than a good old get-together. Pam was a tall, elegant and well-read woman, one who would soon become my dancing partner for the next fifteen years. There's was never a dull moment at any party Pam attended and we soon had our dance routine for our fans. Pam showed such kindness to the animals we rescued, and it wasn't long until she took charge of our poultry and was aptly nicknamed Chicken Pam for services to our feathered friends.

On one occasion at a fundraiser for the animals, Pam and I took to the dance floor of the local curry house. With half the restaurant knowing what was in store for them and the other having no idea, we started to perform our routine. Pam, who had already had a fair share of the vino, was happily gliding across the floor to the sounds of Amy Winehouse's version of 'Valerie'. Our audience loved us, and the atmosphere was electric; we had the restaurant up and dancing. We danced the floor, but then Pam missed my hand to steady and slow her moves, and at what seemed like a hundred miles per hour she hit a large PA system that toppled back and landed on a man eating his vindaloo. The heavy piece of equipment knocked him out cold. Pam may have landed on her bottom, but it was in style and she was up again within seconds and back on the dance floor. The restaurant called an ambulance and the fundraiser came to an unusual end.

One ordinary day caring for the animals, I visited the vet with Remus, our old sheep who suffered from lameness. Whilst injecting Remus with pain relief, Trevor the vet commented that I had more animals than any one of his clients. He asked if we'd ever considered that we were really an animal rescue centre, even if we didn't accept it. He went on to tell me he was the vet to rescue centres with half the numbers of animals and species we took in. I didn't think any more about our conversation until I received my invoice from Trevor, with *Animal Rescue* and my name written on it. We all laughed about this, with no idea that an epic moment in the history of animal rescue in Kent was just about to be witnessed.

A few weeks later, Trevor arrive to do his monthly checks on our old ponies and asked if we liked the 'animal rescue' invoice.

'Everyone had an opinion on the topic of animal rescue and if we did or did not qualify,' I replied. All I was interested in was helping the next needy animal, and I didn't need to be an animal rescue organisation to help the kind of creatures who needed me. Uniforms, leaflets and brands meant nothing to me – I was far too busy saving animals the very animals forgotten by welfare organisations.

'You need to call this place something,' Trevor said, 'it deserves a name.'

'It's like a retreat for animals,' Neil replied, and so our next invoice arrived with *The Retreat* on the top line, followed by *Animal Rescue* and my name.

And so The Retreat Animal Rescue was born just like that, with absolutely no permission from me at all. It's a funny old world because up until The Retreat had a name, I would find the animals needing help but before long they began to find me. Animals and birds of all sorts started to be left at the gate. From horses herded down my drive, chickens in plastic sacks, boxes of sick puppies, piglets, dogs tied up, cats and rabbits in cardboard boxes and small pet rodents in dirty cages, it became a regular problem. Even some very sick animals would be left in the pouring rain. I never turned anyone, away so there was no need to leave animals in danger at the gate.

One bright summer's afternoon I watched a car pull in and, with the engine still running, a man and his dog (a large white saluki) got out. The man threw the dog's ball as far as he could into the surrounding corn field and once the hound took off, he jumped into his car and sped off like a lunatic. Heart in my mouth, I had just witnessed a real-life dumping. I sprinted up the drive hoping to meet the dog on his return. I thought how many times the playful dog had retrieved the ball to the praise of his master. The loyal dog excitedly returned with the ball in his mouth and came running back happy to please his master – a man who was no longer there, a heartless man who seemed to have no understanding of man's best friend, or maybe friendship altogether. I named the beautiful dog Sebastian.

My friendship with Pam and Ian flourished into a partnership where they would love and look after not just the feathered rescues but many of the cats too. One beautiful August morning, Pam broke the news to us that the house next door to them was about to come up for sale – and the next stage of The Retreat's journey was born. The owners wanted a quick sale and being friendly with us, didn't even put the house on the market. The house was covered in ivy and Virginia creeper, giving it character which I loved. Built as a farm worker's house, it had been extended over the years to make a large family home. The semi-detached house needed some love, but this didn't matter to us because love was what this house was going to get, and lots of it. It also had a long narrow shaded garden covered with trees and shrubs which led out to The Retreat.

Living on site with our family of rescued misfits and with the friendship of Pam and Ian next door we would have our own Shangri-La. The number of residents continued to grow and with the new house, our dog numbers reached one hundred and four, as well as ninety cats – and that's without the rest of our rescues. The old recording studio on the side of the house soon became our hospital room for new arrivals.

Our home was the meeting place for our human family too and every Sunday morning friends and family would gather for an epic cooked breakfast made by Neil. All my great-nieces and nephews would be there from Charlie Dogbite, Superdog Alfie, Lillie, JJ and Demi; they loved to meet the latest additions like Abigail the house pig and Eddie and Andrew, two bottle-fed foals. Our friend Lesley from Chislehurst would pop in and fall in love with a new cat to take home to add to her collection.

After breakfast (which was like feeding the five thousand) we would all go for a good dog walk with up to forty dogs at a time for miles across the surrounding countryside. Many of our dogs were what was known as death row dogs, dogs who had no chance anywhere else; Norman the Japanese Akita,

Jasper, Holly, Flossie, Harvey and Jeremy the mad collies, Troy, Richie, Reggie, Nellie and Ben the Rottweilers, Denver, Penny, Dora, Gracey, Kim and Mia the greyhounds, Ronnie the Retriever, Tasha, Edward and Sonny the Labradors, Degas, Whitey, Strippy and Patch (the many beagles), Elvis, Jeremiah Esquire, Tara and Rula (some of the many crosses), Rory, Leo, Bonnie, Prince, Katie and Khan the German shepherds, Truman, Coast, Elf, Kanas, and Andrew and Dante the Great Danes.

On these memorable walks our dogs got to run and swim with the human youngsters to their hearts contents. It wasn't only animals we gave sanctuary too; our home was a constant boarding house for humans who had nowhere else to go. The bedrooms were sometimes turned around like housekeeping staff do in hotel chains. I had somehow combined animal rescue with human hostel too.

CHAPTER ELEVEN

IT'S A GIRL

The subject of having children had occasionally raised its head with Neil and me. We both agreed it was a wonderful idea in theory but in reality it seemed impossible that we could fit anything else into our daily schedule. On a practical and logical note, to have had children would have meant giving up so many hours rescuing and caring for animals, and it would divert crucial funding away from them. Space was also an issue; rooms would have to be given up to provide a bedroom, playrooms and garden space. We were totally amazed at just how parents did it. After many years of deliberating on the subject of children, we decided it would be unworkable if we wanted to continue our rescue work and build a bigger Ark.

Then everything changed in a heartbeat. I had gone along to a party with some friends at Carla's animal sanctuary where Suki my Egyptian goose lived happily. Everyone at the party was having a good time when I arrived, and I said the usual hellos. It wasn't long until a very confident young woman said hi, swigging her glass of wine whilst chewing gum. We started to chat about how I knew the sanctuary and was I an animal lover? Did I have any animals? It emerged that horses were her passion.

Scarlet looked about twenty-five years old and continued

with a mature conversation about her love for equines. I realised immediately that she was a competent horse woman and was sure that this must be her profession. I asked her what she did for a living and was shocked to find out she was still at school. Scarlet was only thirteen and had been expelled from multiple schools for unruly behaviour. I couldn't believe it – she was only thirteen yet seemed so adult and knowledgeable. It wasn't long into our conversation that I worked her out: she was a lovable rogue with a heart of gold, just totally misunderstood. All she wanted was to be with horses. Horses never judged her, they only loved her for who she was.

Our conversation touched on Scarlet's troubled times and I was interested to know what was next for her. Before we parted to talk to other party goers, I handed her The Retreat's number. I told her I could see her getting in more trouble if she didn't sort herself out, and that I wanted to help. She replied that it was her life, and disappeared into the crowd.

It wasn't even two weeks later when I got a phone call from a man saying he was Scarlet's father. Scarlet's parents just couldn't cope with her disruptive behaviour anymore, they had run out of options. I think due to me having thirty-three horses (and rescuing more on a weekly basis), they felt that Scarlet would be better off living with me even if I was a stranger. The very next day, Scarlet was driven to us with very few possessions, and Neil and I now had a daughter – a thirteen-year-old girl who thought she was an adult. Scarlet was full of anger and disappointment and had no gratitude to those trying to help her, and we'd missed the cute baby years of taking first steps and uttering first words, which would build the bond between parent and new-born. We had simply woken up to a teenager in our lives – one who answered back with the venom of a rattlesnake – and we had to work out a plan to accommodate her.

This was not going to be easy, but I could see that beneath the hard veneer Scarlet had a huge heart. In fact, her love for all things horse and dog was our magic wand. Gradually, our plan to let her heal around the animals began to work. We found out it was not a good idea to expect her out of bed when our day started but without fail she would turn up at some stage to help care for the horses, always followed by her canine fan club.

Telling Scarlet not to do something or the word 'no' was also a red rag moment, like day one when I told her not to stroke Bryn, who was the dog equivalent to Scarlet. An elderly dachshund with the fierceness of a lion, he was best left alone and just like Scarlet he hated being told what to do. Against the advice of her new parents, Scarlet bent down to the dog and he clamped his teeth around her hand. She didn't cry easily, but I think maybe her pride was bruised more than her bleeding hand. For a minute or two I saw a different person, one who was really just a kid who needed my help.

When Scarlet was at her best, she was the daughter of all daughters to have but when she was at her worst, she would have tried the patience of a hundred saints. I was the bad cop and Neil was the good cop; I was the one who imposed strict rules on her to ensure her healing continued and her rewards were taking responsibility for certain horses. Scarlet would bring around the wildest of horses with kindness and love. Our time as parents whilst she was growing up presented many problems but applying the same methods to the rehabilitation of our rescues – kindness, friendship, support and a great sense of humour – really did work. Today our non-biological daughter Scarlet is a well-rounded mother to Sebastian. She does her best to help animals when she can and is instilling in Sebastian that kindness to animals really matters, and that wherever you are whatever you are doing it's never too much to be kind to all creatures.

CHAPTER TWELVE

THE INTRUDER

I t was a very cold January evening, the forecast threatening snow and the frost already creeping in. It had been one of those busy rescue days where the calls for help just didn't stop coming. Pam and Ian popped in and Scarlet, Neil, Lewis our live-in and I sat down for a well-deserved meal and bottle of wine. Our open-plan kitchen and dining room were filled with sleepy cats and dogs of all different shapes and sizes – after all, their day had been busy too!

We pondered the day of animals saved and the juggling of places to put them all. We laughed about Scarlet's arguments with Lewis about who should have the front seat and the night drifted on nicely. Pam and Ian's stories of the latest overflow of our cats that had moved in with them and what crazy names they had given them (Winnipeg, Juliet and so on) kept us all laughing. It was about midnight when Pam and Ian left for their not-so-long walk home to next door.

After doing the last head count ensuring that everyone was in, we turned off the lights and went up to bed. An assortment of dogs and cats climbed the stairs with us and filed off into either Scarlet's, Lewis's or our room. Our bedroom was a large room in the loft and had views out the back of The Retreat and the surrounding countryside. The front looked across the fields to a skyline of some of London's tallest buildings. I loved seeing the lights of the Canary Wharf Tower through the naked winter trees, knowing my roots were never too far away. I never tired of these views and how they made an amazing watchtower too.

I read my book for a while and slowly started to fall asleep. I must have been asleep for a few hours when I woke to the distant sound of dogs barking. I laid there for a while whilst I worked out who was barking. I realised I was hearing the voices of Norman the Japanese Akita and Troy the Rottweiler – two of our strongest and most unwelcoming dogs. They both weighed around 65 kilos, and these weren't their *hello* barks I was hearing. Both my wonderful boys had been saved from the needle of euthanasia and rewarded me with unmatched loyalty that only a dog could. They were The Retreat's protectors and would never allow any uninvited person in. Around the children and helpers of The Retreat they were soft and cuddly and showed us only love, but right now they were telling a different story.

I couldn't believe anyone would be outside in the freezing cold and the clock said 3am. I got up and looked out to a clear frosty night. Both Troy and Norman were running around the pond – they were clearly after something, but there couldn't be a person in the pond. I rushed out, thinking maybe a duck had been disturbed. With no shoes on and only my underpants I ran down the stairs and through the house as quietly as I could. I ran up the garden and out towards the pond. The evening's temperatures were below zero. It was a clear night, and now I saw that the dogs were now at the Animal Ambulance vehicle and jumping all over something. I didn't think for one single moment we may be being broken in and it could be someone dangerous. Freezing, I called the excited boys over to me, but they continued to run back to the van. Were they trying to tell me something?

At first it looked like something had fallen out of the passenger door – maybe a sack of feed – and was lying up against the footwell. It was at this stage that I first thought the object was more the shape of a human slumped on the floor but leaning into the van. I couldn't believe it – was he trying to steal the van? He had not noticed me, so I grabbed a broken broom stick and stuck it into his back.

'Don't move,' I yelled in a Hollywood movie voice that even Sylvester Stallone would have been proud of, 'I've got a gun in your back and I'm not afraid to use it. The police are on their way and you're in trouble.'

Now I was shouting, hopefully loud enough for the neighbours to hear. My detainee said nothing and did not move. *My goodness,* I thought shivering to the bone. *I've got no phone, no torch, no shoes…and what if he turns around and sees me only in my tiny blue briefs? I'll be more of a Jackie than a Sylvester Stallone.* The intruder was following my instruction not to move, but nobody was coming to my rescue. What now? Would I be found the following day frozen to death in the most unflattering underpants ever? It was down to me to get the intruder (and hopefully my only one) to the house.

'Are you alone?' I yelled to him, still holding my wooden firearm to his back.

'No, we're all here,' the man said. 'All of us, we're here everywhere, and my wife's in the back making tea.'

A total madman, I thought. I'd have preferred the intruder to just stand and fight me. This man could have been concealing his very own real firearm or machete in the footwell. I noticed he also had no shoes and socks on, and his trousers were very badly torn. Why did he not try to get up? He was also soaking wet and was shivering more than I was. In pure survival mode so I didn't die in the most unflattering underwear ever I looked around for some inspiration. Both dogs sat by my side and awaited their next command, but I was out of ideas. The nearest thing to me was an old-fashioned wheelbarrow, the sort that people gardened with after the war. It had a very slim almost bicycle wheel and a small shallow metal tray on top, and for this reason it was never used by the team.

I stepped back and grabbed the horticultural antique and pushed it alongside him. With another push of my theatrical firearm prop into his back, I shouted to the man to get up and get in, pushing him towards the poor excuse of a wheelbarrow. To my shear amazement, he stood upright and without the bat of an eyelid climbed into the tiny tray on wheels. Now what would I do? I lifted the handles and with Troy and Norman running by my side I made my way back to the house, shouting for help. My poor feet, not only frozen but sore from pebbles and things underfoot, could not take much more. The intruder held on with both hands and never once questioned the fact he was being transported in a wheelbarrow by a man in ill-fitting underwear.

On pulling up at the back of the house Neil came running down the garden shouting to me: 'Billy, I think you're having a breakdown.'

'I've found a man, he's in the wheelbarrow!' I cried back. Neil stared blankly at me as the intruder climbed out of his chariot driven by a half-naked servant and proceeded to walk into the electric fence.

'Please, turn off the electric, please,' he cried out, breaking his silence at last. By this time the house was waking and Scarlet and Lewis were coming to help. In the spotlights, I could see that the intruder was a confused older man, possibly in his eighties. A very upright and polite chap, he apologised for disturbing us; there was obviously a problem for him to be out so late at night in the freezing cold. Scarlet got him into the house whilst Neil made him a bowl of hot water to put his poor feet into and a strong cup of tea. Lewis brought him clean socks, a blanket and towels. The team made him feel welcome and even gave him a piece of Neil's homemade Battenberg cake.

I called 999 and asked for police and when asked the problem I explained I discovered an intruder climbing into my van. The police controller asked if I had managed to actually see the intruder and if I could describe him.

'Yes,' I said, 'he's sitting on my sofa right now!' The controller asked how he had got from the van to the sofa, and I explained that I had told him to get into the wheelbarrow and wheeled him to the house.

'Really sir,' the controller commented, 'so what's he doing now?'

'He's got his feet in a hot bowl of water and he's drinking his tea and eating cake,' I replied. To my astonishment the controller asked me what cake it was.

'Bloody Battenberg,' I yelled. 'I need some assistance now!'

It was now 4:30am and the controller thought I was one of the many nightly nuisance callers. 'I know this sounds crazy, but it's true and I need your help.'

At 5:30am with still no sight or sound of a patrol car, I called 999 again to get my second baffled controller. The controller asked if the intruder had run off or disappeared now.

'No,' I replied.

The controller then asked if I could see him clearly, and what he was doing.

'My patience is running dry,' I firmly replied. 'He's having a chat about the war and he thinks it's 1944.' The intruder had taken no umbrage at the dogs ripping his trousers or losing his shoes in the pond when escaping the jaws of Troy and Norman. Oddly enough he seemed to be enjoying the chat and company. A police car finally arrived just after 6am and out came two guys with grins on their faces.

'Has he gone?' was the first thing they asked me.

'No,' I said, knocking the smiles off their faces. 'He's still sitting on the sofa eating his third piece of cake.'

'Battenberg,' they laughed. Apparently, the whole station thought it was a joke.

The man was pleased to see the police and told them all about his evening, that he and his wife were collecting hot water to prepare dinner. He praised the bravery of our dogs and the kindness of our hospitality. He then told the police his full name and address and they managed to contact his son. The police confirmed our fears that he had wandered out of his home in the early hours. Our nightmare of an evening was compensated by the fact Stanley the intruder was not injured and he had actually enjoyed his tea and Battenberg cake time in the house with us all. The moral of tonight's tale was the sadness of loneliness and its magical cure, companionship. Scarlet once again without even knowing it had shown remarkable kindness and support to Stanley just like she did with those horses needing help.

CHAPTER THIRTEEN

FRIENDS

Rescuing animals has driven me for most of my life. I've never been interested in making money out of animals like boarding animals, riding lessons, breeding or selling their products. I've only ever wanted to help them and take nothing in return. Rescuing animals has led me to meet my best friends, and that's been reward enough.

My journeys overseas helping street animals gave me many friendships, two of which stood the test of time. My earliest was a woman called Violet who was helping dogs in Istanbul, Turkey, but lived in Kent on the East coast. At the time of hearing about Violet I was helping dogs in the western coastal resorts of Turkey and heard she needed some additional help. I took the long tedious and uncomfortable coach journey of over ten hours to Istanbul to meet her and hopefully lend a hand with the dogs.

Violet was a tall thin older woman maybe in her seventies. She was deeply tanned and very agile for her years. Although an authentic animal person, you could feel her anger. Life had been very cruel to her. She had had everything but lost it due to greedy Turkish lovers. Her husband died early and left her financially well cared for. Her daughter had married young and was no longer in touch. The street dogs filled her lonely hours and were now her life and all she was interested in.

Whether she pleased or offended you, Violet only spoke the truth, and this alone had led to her harsh reputation. She had very little time for humans, even the ones who wanted to help animals, and was slowly running out of helpers.

Apparently, Violet liked me before we even met. Our long (expensive) phone calls had won her over, my passion and enthusiasm for helping the neediest of animals had struck a chord with her. Her few remaining dedicated and loyal helpers were shocked to hear this; Violet was not known for making friends, especially male ones. By her own admission she was a man-hater.

When she met me at the coach station she greeted me with half a bottle of water and a sandwich, and our friendship was sealed because food won me over every time. I stepped off the coach tired, hot and a little unenthusiastic, and spotted the legendary dog woman standing in the shade.

'Hi, I'm Violet,' she acknowledged me from underneath her vast sunhat. 'I'm sure you're hungry.' I refused the sandwich, not knowing it was vegan, and with a look that could beat Medusa in turning people to stone she pushed it back, telling me it was just lettuce, salt and olive oil. Insulted by my assumption, she walked off.

Violet was a vegan too and had been one for over five decades. Who was I to doubt her compassionate sandwich-making skills? We had a few more professional struggles, but these only cemented our bond. Our ideas were very different, and she would stand her ground as firmly as I would. We often locked horns and neither would give in. In the end we would always make up over whiskey and Dolmas, one of our favourite Turkish foods. Violet would always drink me under the table and never seemed worse for wear the next morning. I eventually proved my worth whether in blood and sweat or just outsmarting the old girl on a new idea to trap a difficult dog. Some of these dogs she had been trying to catch for weeks who cleverly avoided her capture, but I proudly caught in hours.

Violet could not ignore my talents in catching dogs, and I loved to see her face when I brought her the latest one. The ground-breaking work she did for the dogs was not easy. She suffered physical and verbal abuse from locals who didn't care for an outsider telling them what to do with the street animals. Violet never ever gave up or gave in she was focused on her end result: 'no more suffering'. She had her mantra and would often comment to me when the going got tough that 'we don't sweat that small stuff'. She was an incredible mentor who taught me so much. When faced with no feasible solution to a dog in trouble she never gave up but simply drove the 1,800 miles back to Kent to the safety of her canine compound.

We continued to work together overseas and when she was home I would come to visit, and we would rescue animals at home in true Violet style. Her pack of crazy rescued Turkish hounds were a pleasure to meet up and walk on the beaches of Dymchurch and Camber Sands. One outstanding rescue story of ours was when she asked me to help her on a rescue to catch a wallaby that she said was living rough in some woods. Violet briefed me the landowner would be glad to see the back of the wallaby before his dogs killed it. The only problem was the dreadfully cruel farm next door was trying to claim ownership of her.

When it came to an animal in need Violet knew no fear – after all she carried the most dangerous weapon of all: her tongue. On arrival at the site we walked across the fields and into a small wooded area where immediately I sighted the unusual creature. The wallaby was glad to see us. She was incredibly tame and a cheeky character. Violet led us back to her car, the two of us dropping the monkey nuts in front of the wallaby like Hansel and Gretel laying breadcrumbs whenever the wallaby stopped following us. She was easier than most Turkish dogs to catch, we laughed.

Amidst distant shouts of *'leave it alone, that's ours'*, Violet kept her head down and continued to encourage her to keep following. The wallaby was very friendly but sadly in poor shape. We rested for a while because she was weak, and I cleaned her eyes of dry dirt. She even held your hand.

'These rednecks are nothing compared to my run-ins with the Turkish police,' Violet commented. *Poor Turkish police*, I thought. The landowner came over and told us the poor thing needed to see a vet before she dies. When we got to the car Violet got a towel out and rubbed the wallaby's body clean. I noticed she was bigger than I thought for a wallaby and we joked that she could be a kangaroo.

The landowner's wife came out and said the people trying to catch her were all out on the road. Violet, never one to be put off helping animals, even in the most intimating of situations which I had myself witnessed many of times on the streets of Istanbul, quietly signalled me to load the girl into the back of the car.

'Violet, others will see her,' I warned.

'Not with what I've got in mind,' Violet said with one of

123

her cold looks. We lifted our new rescue up onto the back seat of her old purple Suzuki 4x4 Samurai soft top jeep.

'Now what's the plan?' I said, and Violet instructed me to get into the back with her. Violet took off her ancient mac and within seconds dressed the wallaby in her overcoat, turning up the sleeves. She pulled her famous vast sun hat, which she had been wearing the day I first met her in Istanbul, out from under the seat and popped it on the wallaby's head, arranging it over her ears. I was worried the hat would fly off and expose our incognito fugitive, so we tied it on with one of Violet's scarves. How would we ever escape with an overdressed wallaby who I thought looked like the Queen Mother? It just seemed so ridiculous. A rather perplexed wallaby sat eating the monkey nuts and we took off.

Up ahead on the road were the eight or so rednecks looking for her. Violet ordered me to put my arm around her and look deep into her eyes. I did, but her bad breath kept me at arm's length because I'm not good with smells until midday. I'm not sure who was more fascinated by whom. She looked so at home sitting in the back of a car I wondered how often she got a ride. With the pair of us sitting in the back creating a happy love scene, Violet weaved through the bounty hunters, giving them a casual but encouraging wave. They stared into the back at us and even gave us a wave.

Pulling away in her soft top jeep, it was the first time I'd ever seen Violet smile, and I'm sure she almost broke into a laugh. She remarked that the wallaby dressed like that reminded her of the famous Audrey Hepburn taxi whistle scene in *Breakfast At Tiffany's*; all she needed now was a pair of sunglasses. Safe at last, our newly rescued wallaby was now christened Audrey. She remained fully clothed for the rest of the journey until safe inside Violet's compound.

Violet and I dined out on that story for many years later and I proudly read it as part of her incredible eulogy after her death. She was a true hero until her last breath.

Another ambassador for animals I met on overseas projects was Liz of Catastrophes Cat Rescue. It was arranged that I would meet Liz 'The Cat Lady' at Gatwick airport to travel to the South East of Spain and help the street cats. Liz, like so many of us, had dedicated her life to offering the neediest of cats a lifeline. The very old ones or those with behavioural issues would be welcomed to a beautiful and happy life at her sixteenth century country home in the Sussex countryside. She took the ones the other cat shelters didn't want or would have killed.

I had a standard travel plan that included a unique luggage system for neutering projects: I would take two animal hospital baskets which were made of wire and roughly the size of cat carriers. These were very useful on our projects. I would fill black bags inside the baskets of the absolute minimum I would use, and the rest would be filled with anything we needed for the cats. My luggage was often the topic of conversation when checking in at the airport with the airline staff.

I had agreed to give Liz a call when I arrived at the airport so we could finally meet each other. Having previously heard of the amazing work she did for cats, I was thrilled to finally get the chance to meet and work with such a respected rescuer. Animal people seem to share the common problem of punctuality so of course we were both late.

When I finally arrived inside the busy airport I plonked my stuff down and got my phone out. A quick glance around confirmed that there were no cat ladies on my radar. Over the years I had met my share of crazy cat ladies all pretty cliched with the classic fake fur hat, heavy overcoat full of cat hair and thrown-up munchies stuck to the back, plus the sweet smell of ammonia lingering where you could tell they had been. Many wore poor-fitting flat shoes with the usual cat mess up the side and cat scratched leggings or frayed seventies flowery skirts that were all obtained years ago from the local bring and buy sales – and of course, the number one cat lady accessory: a pull-along trolley-bag on wheels. My cat ladies were never the twinset-and-pearl brigade I'd heard so much about that frequented national cat shows.

I looked up Liz's number and at the same time noticed an immaculately dressed Joan Collins lookalike (or maybe the real thing) applying her lipstick – 'Frosty Rose' – opposite me. She was travelling too with a wealth of good luggage, piles of it. I reckoned her shoe collection would give Imelda Marcos's renowned collection of three thousand designer shoes a run for its money. I smiled and wondered what far-off destination she was travelling to, Bora Bora in the French Polynesia with its clear blue seas or maybe Princess Margaret's hideaway island of Mustique and miles of Sandy beaches? Wherever her travels would take her I'm sure it was more catwalk than cat work. I called and waited for Liz to answer her phone. At that moment, 'Joan Collins' took her phone from her bag, speaking as the phone on the other end of the line answered.

'Hi, is that Billy?' the woman opposite – and the voice on the phone – said in complete synchronisation. At this point, 'Joan Collins' noticed my baskets and summoned me over with a dignified wave.

'There you are,' she said with a laugh, and hung up.

Gobsmacked, I waved back and approached the most peculiar cat woman of our time. To my amazement there was no smell of ammonia; when I kissed her only the signature smell of Marilyn Monroe's Chanel No. 5. Both Liz and I had the totally wrong perception of each other. She had been expecting an old man called Bill with a flat cap and bicycle clips, when in fact I was just thirty. I thought she was going to be a dear old lady who really needed a bath – how wrong we both were.

This trip marked the start of a partnership that lasted fifteen years travelling Europe to help the neediest of street strays. Liz's partner Alan would also come along to enjoy the many antics of our field surgery when he wasn't saving orangutans and sloth bears around the world. There was never a dull moment travelling with Liz and I'm glad to say it resulted in many thousands of animals being helped.

One of our most memorable trips was when we travelled to mountainous Northern Greece to neuter the street animals. We set up in a village on the Pelion peninsula and with the help of a local woman called Yarka, we set out to do our best for the animals of the area. Yarka worked very differently to Liz and I, and it soon started to cause problems. Yarka was obviously used to getting her own way and could be difficult if the team had different ideas. Both Liz and I were of the same ilk; we worked slow and steady, so each animal got a tailored healthcare plan for whatever they needed most. Yarka wanted the maximum number of cats neutered per day with no other care. I would be the one negotiating a middle way between our strong-willed cat ladies Liz versus Yarka.

One day we were driving the narrow and snake-like mountain roads and, me being an overly cautious driver, I was not getting out of third gear. Liz was in the passenger seat going through her bag full of index cards filled with the details of our trapping locations and the cats themselves, then freezer bags full with different currency from previous trips. She would also reapply her Frosty Rose lipstick, taking her mind of the sheer mountainside drop. It always intrigued me for such a stylish traveller that in her gold handbag was a world full of her idiosyncrasies and a tell-tale sign of her lack of trust in technology. She loved pen and paper and her handbag held the answers to all her questions.

Whilst driving the winding roads where I couldn't see around the next bend and fearing for our own safety on the edge of the mountain roads, I had slowed down even further due to a holiday coach in front of us. Yarka insisted I speed up and take over the coach ahead – crazy, I thought. I explained that I could not do it, and at this point she leant into the front of the car and with waves of her fist to the coach in front and bellows of, 'Bill faster, faster Bill, overtake Bill, come on Bill', she frustrated herself with my self-preservation. Liz would fight my corner and calmly responded, 'Billy you're the driver, you drive as fast or as slow as you feel safe to do and don't worry about her in the back. She's not in charge and she's not driving'.

Yarka ignored Liz and continued with her bellows and Liz ignored Yarka with her calm comments supporting my driving until we reached our destination. A huffy Yarka jumped out, swearing under her breath, and Liz pulled out the appropriate index card to assess the rescue work needed. I only hoped there was another way back to avoid the mountains and the craziness of Yarka.

Neutering was an important part of our work because it reduced the number of animals competing for the scarce resources available, plus in certain parts of Europe people were happy to poison cats and dogs like we poison rats at home. Poisoning is a terrible death for all creatures. Our clinics were not just a conveyor belt of neutering – that's not what our team was about. If a cat needed a dental or a leg amputation, they would get it. The animals that we trapped and arrived at the clinics with would get a five-star service and were treated no diffident to animals arriving at the vets at home.

One poor old cat needed some additional nursing after having to have a full dental. Liz immediately set up a convalescing area in her room and cared for Hope the cat night and day. Another little creature, a dog called Rula, was really struggling after a complicated operation. Generally, we kept the patients for about two days and then released back to their own areas. A lesson we all had to learn was that they had to go back, since the areas we worked in often had no sanctuaries or rescue centres. Street life or no life were the only two options for most of these animals. For both Hope and Rula this would not be the case; they needed much more than the streets could provide for them.

Each day we would see signs of both our little fighters getting better, but not as fast as we would have liked. On day five and running out of time, Rula seemed to have turned a corner in her slow recovery. Today seemed to be the day she would return to life behind the travel agent. I drove down to the town with Rula on my lap, just like being at home in the UK. I had a pile of blankets and food to leave with Yolanda who would carry on caring for her.

I arranged the small area behind the shop where Rula had lived for three years. I remembered being told that last year someone had poisoned all her tiny puppies and she too was very sick for weeks after the sad event. I felt sick, thinking how she had grown to trust me in only five days. I made her bed and filled the bowls with clean water and food and left her to eat. My eyes welled up and with a heavy heart I slipped into the car and started to drive off. I wasn't going to cry. Rula had only known the freedom of the streets and who was I to change that?

I was just pulling onto the main road when I glanced in the rear-view mirror and saw a little ball of curly white hair chasing the car. I couldn't believe it – she was running for her life, an absolute plea for help, and she must have thought I wasn't listening. I pulled over and opened the driver's door at which she positively jumped up onto my lap and licked my face. Looking at me like, 'Have you forgotten something, Dad?'. Was I just like the guy who threw the ball into the corn field leaving Sebastian the Saluki heartbroken when he ran out to find his owner gone? What was I thinking, leaving her when I knew the score with people poisoning dogs in the town? Taking her back to the UK would not only cost a fortune in quarantine but would also take months, I had reasoned. Having regularly brought back animals from Europe before the Pet Passport System was up and running, I knew the cost all too well.

I walked back into the clinic with Rula and explained to Liz that I had to take her back home with me, I couldn't leave her.

'That's fantastic,' an emotional Liz replied. 'Because that's what I'm doing with Hope the cat too.'

The local vet prepared Rula and Hope to travel and this time Liz and I happily paid at the veterinary clinic, so everything was above board. It was a beautiful morning to set off to Volos Airport, and Liz and I had our new friends safely inside their new travel cages. Volos Airport had recently been in the news with tales of UK plane spotters being government spies. There was lots of interest in British travellers but oddly enough not the crazy A-Team (that's A for animal). The atmosphere was relaxed and friendly, and we passed through the airport quickly. Yolanda from the travel agent was with us and reassured us not to worry about our fluffy travel companions and that her cousin was today's pilot. We just followed the larger than life travel rep who seemed to know everyone.

Yolanda kissed her cousin at the stairs to the plane and Liz and I shook his hand. Memories of an Egyptian incident on the tarmac came flooding back but this time things would be different, after all it was not Tutankhamun on a Harley Davison that signed the export paperwork in Volos. Rula and Hope were taken from us and loaded under the plane. They looked comfortable, so we happily boarded the aircraft. It had been an exhausting time and we was glad to see the back of Yarka of Greece.

The plane ride went smoothly, and we landed in time for my dad's birthday meal that day. We rushed through passport control to the baggage reclaim area and waited for a million pieces of Liz's luggage and our Hope and Rula. Liz had noticed the airport police with their semi-automatic weapons were speaking on radios and looking very interested in us. Liz smiled at them; maybe they had mistaken her for the internationally acclaimed actress Joan Collins, just like I did when I first spotted her. They then made their way over to us.

'Miss Varney and Mr Thompson,' they said sternly.

'Yes?' we replied.

'Can you come this way please.'

We were escorted to an interview room in the Animal Reception Area and interviewed under caution for three hours. Apparently, we were in the middle of an International Aviation Incident caused by an illegal landing. The airline we had flown home on were not licensed to import or handle livestock. A technicality, or so we thought, because we were here now. Or would we need to fly back to Greece?

The interviewers seemed to be blaming us for the incident, maybe wanting to get their own back at Greece for the latest arrests of British plane spotters, even though this had nothing to do with us. We were told that the airline could sue, and Hope and Rula could be confiscated or worse. With the famous words of Violet in my head – 'we don't sweat the small stuff' – I tried to be positive. I remembered my dear friends Laura and Dean had just started a quarantine facility and that they would vouch for us and offer the furries a place of safety until all could be sorted out. I handed over Dean and Laura's number.

Thankfully with Lizzie's famous 'airport face' and her turning out of endless freezer bags filled with cash, the interviewers started to soften even maybe started to understand, even if they were a little baffled. Liz's freezer bags were no bribe, just a show of our vulnerabilities. We were not international money launderers or gangland criminals, hijackers or terrorists, just a couple of ordinary people with big hearts. They soon realised it was not our mistake; we were genuinely trying to save animals and not pull the wool over border force's eyes. We were just two innocent animal rescue people doing our best to get animals to safety.

Hope and Rula would have to go off to the quarantine facility for the next six months. For street animals quarantine is a seven-star hotel, a place of safety with the best food and care you can get. It would be like us checking into the spa for six months unlike the streets they came from where hunger, fear, torment and death are daily obstacles. The months flew by and soon Liz and I could pick up our new family members and take them home. Life had really just started for these two precious strays...

A couple of times a month I would attend the local livestock market to monitor the practices of those selling everything and anything. Sevenoaks livestock market attracted some real rednecks and they would turn up with all sorts of baby animals to be sold. Many of the unsold ducklings, chicks and rabbits would end up in the litter bins in the car park. There were even times unsold calves and lambs were discarded like rubbish rather than being taken back. I was always ready with pet carriers, bottled water and food to help the neglected.

Once, I noticed a single lamb about a week old all alone in a pen. *Unbelievable,* I thought, *who would bring her to market?* She was the cutest little creature, about half the size of a cocker spaniel. She was nervous and couldn't settle. The bidding started at £6. Nobody seemed to want her, so to my surprise and against everything I stood for, I waved my hand to seal the deal.

This started an instant war between myself and a woman dressed in full country clothing of waxed coat and hat, green wellies, who seemed at home in the centre of such an uncaring environment. I eventually won the bidding and baby Jessica the lamb was coming home with me. When I went to the pen to collect her I was followed by Mrs Country Clothing herself. The woman giving me a scathing look, skilfully holding a rolled-up cigarette in the side of her mouth whilst she talked. She mumbled something to which I ignored, and she raised her voice.

'What are you going to do with her then?' she asked arrogantly.

'Love her, unlike you would have,' I replied, using one of my best *who do you think you are* faces.

'Where are you taking her?' the woman demanded.

'To my sanctuary,' I replied through gritted teeth.

'Sanctuary?' she said. 'What, an animal sanctuary?'

'Yes, an animal sanctuary,' I replied in my best patronising voice.

The woman's reply was not what I expected – Mrs Country Clothing proceeded to tell me she also had an animal sanctuary and was in fact not normally dressed like this but was trying to fit in with the livestock market theme. At first, I wasn't convinced she was telling the truth. She followed me as I carried Jessica the lamb to the car, and we started to chat about our first impressions of each other.

'Anyway, I'm Marion,' she introduced herself. By this point I was starting to like her. She told me that over near Paddock Wood she had an animal sanctuary and small garden nursery called FRIENDS. Not only was she good at role-playing, she was extremely eloquent in her argument for a kinder world. The more we chatted the more I liked her. Her red hair and bright eyes projected a zest that I just knew were more than skin deep. We decided to meet for a coffee and catch up in two weeks' time. We exchanged numbers and agreed she would come over to mine to see how Jessica the lamb were getting on and take a look at The Retreat. Marion called me that night and we laughed about everything from families, animal rescue, TV cookery shows, witches and business ideas. From that day on we never looked back. A friendship sealed over the fate of a tiny lamb named Jessica.

Two weeks and a day later Marion drove down The Retreat's drive with a tiny ten-day-old calf on the front seat of her Citroen. The tiny female calf at just ten days old was being sold for £12. Apparently, her beautiful patterned brown and white skin was ideal for making mittens and she would have been in the freezer that very day. We called her Jill in memory of Jill Phipps who lost her life fighting for calves, and she was our first ever cow. She was such a joy, the real apple of all our eyes, and everyone loved her. To my great nieces and nephews, she became Auntie Jill; a real interspecies family had begun.

Marion had amazing maternal skills. She could hand-rear any creature from baby bats to lambs and calves – everything flourished under her spell, just like our friendship. We called each other most days and tried to meet as often as possible. Oddly enough, our views on many topics were the complete opposite of one another, but we never had an argument or fallout. We were cosmic twins or similar fairyland family members. Marion and I had a brother and sister relationship an eternal bond that would never be broken.

We both loved to dance and some very late Friday nights after our work was done, we would scrub up and venture out. We would end up in a trendy gay bar in London at a foam party having the time of our lives. We were always the last to leave. Serval times, Marion lost her shoes in the sky-high foam like a real-life Cinderella and would return home shoeless. Other Friday nights, Liz, Marion and I would meet a few other rescue workers and end up on the dance floor of The Norbury Hotel near Croydon London where we would let our hair down and dance 'til dawn. Philosophical debates kept us chatting through the nights on rescues.

We talked about everything from afterlife, politics, organic gardening, the end of the world to our favourite holiday destination and where we would live when we were old. Marion's uniqueness was showcased when I visited her once and in her living area she had her eighty-year-old mother Harriet singing the *Hokey Cokey*, a three-eared calf, a three-legged lurcher and a three-legged chicken, all cosy and safe. My friendship with this amazing pioneer grew stronger week by week, month by month, year by year.

I proudly asked Marion to be a witness at Neil's and my

civil ceremony and asked if she would do a bit of a speech because I knew she would make everyone laugh with her incredible tales of animal rescue, and of course she agreed. The day of the ceremony came, and Truman the Great Dane and Bryn the Dachshund wore the same pink ties as Neil and me. During her touching speech of the birth of our friendship and our blessed meeting at the livestock market in the sheep pens, her deep feelings of love and union towards me made everyone cry including my dad and both the registrars. With not a single dry eye in the room Greta's playlist of 'Get Happy' by Judy Garland lifted everyone's mood and an explosion of smiles as wide as a rainbow celebrated our togetherness.

Marion was logical but spiritual; a very deep person who was loved closely by those closest to her. She was a protector and a giver. The years passed and although our meet-ups became less and less frequent we never missed a good old catch up on the phone. Marion never lost her zest for helping the underdog. Sadly, after twenty-one years of friendship a heart-breaking sudden ending was forced upon our collaboration. Marion had a terrible accident at home where she fell down the stairs. She never regained consciousness and after several long weeks in hospital she passed away. I visited her up to four times a week at King's College Hospital and I sat and recounted our rescue work together and the times we danced the night away. We had often laughed that we were the Bonnie and Clyde of animal rescue, outlaws. I'd leave the ward each time not knowing if I'd get another chance to tell her I loved her, whisper 'Goodnight my Bonnie' and kiss her head.

I knew she could hear me. I could see it in her eyes, but she wanted to go so badly. In true Marion style she would have to go when she was ready and not before. Life's never been the same for me since she left – friendships like ours are a rare phenomenon, like the magic of shooting stars and rainbows: a higher blessing that doesn't come along every day.

CHAPTER FOURTEEN

A FLAGSHIP PROJECT

Our move to an old dairy farm in High Halden, Kent, in 2012 would enable us to help more animals with the additional space. The beautiful farm had a history of doing whatever it could to survive – this mostly included anti animal practises of pig, sheep and dairy farming. Later, it became a scrapyard and then sat unused for some time. The property got its name Brickyard Farm from the days when the clay beneath the land was excavated and used for brick making. The layout and existing infrastructure would not only accommodate the work we were already doing for animals but also make room for the public to come and see their donations in action in support of our life-saving work.

Our plan was to create a visitor-friendly site with cafe, shops, free parking and entry, as well as a trail where our visitors could wander around in the peace and quiet and experience our residents on their healing journey. It was a long hard search to find the right premises but when I saw Brickyard Farm, I knew it was the one. With its organic meadows, hundreds of mature oak trees literally hundreds of years old and plenty of natural water it ticked all the boxes. The barns, stables and old dairy sheds would all be useful. There were buildings suitable for hospital and recovery areas, ample winter yards for our large residents to come into, and some extra room for car parking spaces. The lovely old farmhouse would house us and our rescue team.

Brickyard Farm becoming the home to The Retreat would address the history of the bad and negative energy on site and create a paradise for all who lived there. The move would have never been possible without the kindness of a few equally passionate and excellent people, namely Mum, Dad, Lil, Eddy, Richard, Sue B, Pat and Peter whose continued support is the foundation of today's flagship project. Little did I know how our work would increase just by moving fifty miles. The move had not only landed us in the middle of the Kentish horse crisis but also put us in between two farms responsible for harrowing scenes of the worst cruelty.

The Kent horse crisis was an explosion of poorly managed sites all over Kent where horses were indiscriminately bred without any management. These horses lived in areas with very little resources so pregnant mares could not support the baby growing inside them and many were just found dead. Over and inbreeding was commonplace. Foals born male and the wrong colours were just dumped to die, or their mothers were removed so they would just starve to death.

There is cruelty to animals everywhere and the malice of man is never that far from any of us, but this book is about kindness and what we can all do to help animals rather than the saddest of rescue tales. I'm convinced that most people want to live a kind life at one with the natural world and not harm animals. This book shows you that wherever you are whatever you are doing there's always room to help animals.

Our new centre is a meeting place for anyone wanting to do their best for animals. Over the next few years we worked hard to build the infrastructure so we could open our gates to the public. Tree planting was a top priority too and each autumn I would try to plant new hedgerows and trees around the site. I harvested my own willow sticks and found this a productive way to maximise tree planting. Willow sticks can just be pushed into the ground without roots and within a season you have instant trees – a great winter treat for any animal to munch on.

One clear but cold Saturday in December I gathered my hundred willow sticks (about three foot in length) to use. Today I would plant a group of willows around one side of the terrapin lake. I was happily pushing them firmly in around the lake one by one. I was using my body weight to push the sticks in, hanging over the lake's bank, when one suddenly snapped. I was too far down to regain my balance and fell in slow motion towards the water. I had so many layers on including my hat, scarves, gloves and wellies I thought I'd drown. I went into the water headfirst with an almighty splash. It was freezing and the cloudy water filled my mouth, eyes, ears and wellies.

I came up and tried to catch my breath. I then tried my hardest to climb up the bank but the dogs, happy to see their silly soaked dad, kept knocking me back in. I felt so stupid and hoped no one had spotted me. Freezing, I crawled out up a muddy bank and headed for the house, embarrassed. I made my way to the front of the house which we never used, so no one would see just how stupid I had been because I'd never live it down if they did. I reached the secluded front door where a large hedge surrounded the hidden vegetable garden. Here I could strip off the wet, muddy and stinky clothes before I entered the house and was scolded. Then, all I needed to do was run up the stairs to the shower.

I struggled to get my boots off with the water inside creating a suction, but I fought on. I threw my wet hat, gloves and coat to the floor. I pulled the soaked heavy jumper and t-shirt over my head and dropped them onto the pile of wet clothes. I eventually got the boots off and now just in my pants and socks I whipped off my sodden pants and lifted my leg and pulled at the first sock. Leaning back on the front door I tried harder to get the clinging sock off. Not a pretty sight, cold, wet and naked apart from two odd socks, I thought, if anyone could see me now. Teeth chattering and shaking with the cold, I was sure there was no chance of that. One last attempt at pulling my socks off or I would have to go in because I couldn't stop shivering. At this point the number two Ashford to Tenterden bus went past with excited shoppers sitting upstairs ready to see if they could get a glimpse of the rescued residents at The Retreat. The upper decks were full of people staring into The Retreat and there I was. The shocked look on their faces as I nakedly wrestled with my wet socks was unforgettable. Red faced, I ran up the stairs only wearing my socks and jumped into a hot shower without taking them off. What would they all have thought?

Tree planting continued with the rest of the progress at the centre. New cattle areas and winter yards to keep our herds of horses were created. Our wildlife hospital and cattery appeared followed by new enclosures to house our disabled residents. We created car parking and toilets, then visitor paths to welcome the public. Cafe, shop and holiday lodges were set up to support our many residents. This was all ready by 2015 to welcome our supporters.

By the time of our official opening, The Retreat was already responsible for saving tens of thousands of the neediest creatures: ex-battery hens and broiler meat chickens, fancy and common chooks and ornamental waterfowl, factory farmed rabbits, quails and ducks, sheep, pigs and cattle who escaped the slaughterhouse by the skin of their teeth, discarded horses, donkeys, mules and goats, street cats and dogs from around the world and unwanted pets. We also took in injured wildlife, small domestic 'pets' like mice, rats, chinchillas, hamsters, ferrets and guinea pigs, plus racing pigeons, parrots, aviary birds large and small, reptiles, aquatics and exotics. We welcomed them all.

I once got a phone call from a journalist working on a story to free three-and-a-half thousand factory farmed ducks. The egg farm had gone bust and the owner was sending the poor ladies to slaughter if he couldn't find them a home. I didn't have to think about it; I said that The Retreat would have them all, every last one. The Retreat's team hatched a plan (if you excuse the pun) and I gained a new nickname, 'Billy Big Mouth', for saying yes without thinking where we might put all those ducks. We had a network of supporters ready to ferry the ducks to our centre, and then the new homes waiting to collect them.

The day started early with a team at the duck farm collecting the birds and bringing them to The Retreat in large batches. It was a long day, but everyone worked so hard to save every last worn-out little lady. It was a hot day which worried us with the transport, but we had no other option. One duck arrived overheated from the journey and lacked any life. The limp little body was handed to me and I filled a bucket of cold water and slowly lowered her into it. To our surprise, the little lifeless creature started to lift her head after a few minutes. I took her straight to the treatment area and we called her Cinzia after the woman who transporter her. Today, many years later Cinzia and partner Nico now run a rabbit rescue and Cinzia the duck still happily lives with us.

After the majority of ducks left us for new homes, we were left with seven hundred and fifty of the most needy. These ladies were not waterproof due to living life in a barn for their whole life with no access to water for swimming, just rubber nipple water-ports. Before we could allow the ducks their freedom to swim on the open waters of The Retreat, we would have to work hard to waterproof each one. Each duck needed their preening gland activated to oil their feathers in preparation for the great swim, just like my Egyptian goose Suki all those years ago. It was a sight for sore eyes: Seven hundred and fifty ducks walking up and down the drive before we allowed them to swim. Finally, their big day came and out they went to the lake.

After a few false alarms with a few ducks in the front row being pushed into the water by the masses behind, the bravest of the bunch eventually ventured in. With heads dunked and wings flapping, the girls' instincts soon caught up. To see seven hundred and fifty ducks with smiles on their faces was a very happy moment in rescue even if it wasn't that easy to get them in for bed later that day.

Now The Retreat is a centre open from 12-4pm on Thursdays, Fridays, Saturdays and Sundays from March to

December, we have become a pilgrimage for those who care deeply about justice for our fellow Earth-sharers. Our team of devoted animal carers, trustees and managers Scott and Rose are our magic wand of success. We also have our fair share of celebrities who visit, from Peter Egan, Evanna Lynch, Paul O'Grady, Hollywood A-lister Rooney Mara and Jasmine Harman who is now our patron. Influencers including Karin Rigers of VeggieVision TV, Whispers Red the ASMR artist, Joey Carbstrong, Abbie MMNXSON tattoo artist and Vegan Food UK all sing The Retreat's praises. The Retreat also has many dedicated supporters who come a few times a week, whatever the weather, to support the centre. It's a coming together of good people with kind ideas who all have their own audiences to plant the seeds of change for a better world.

I've made a million great friendships from those who come far and wide to visit my dream come true, a long way from my plastic farm set, that's now a reality. It's a wonderful surprise when family turns up and are already members of the vegang like my Aunty Rosie and Aunty Janette and Patrick; it shows you just how far we have all come in giving something back to planet Earth.

A touching moment for me during 2020 the year of COVID-19 and lockdowns came during the summer when we were lucky enough to reopen. One of our team had just finished doing a show-around for a young couple and I arrived with Lil in the cafe at the same time they were washing their hands. The young guy in his mid-twenties came over and asked if my sister and I had been nursery teachers years ago. To our total surprise the gentle young man had been one of our students from the age of one years old to five and had miraculously remembered my kindness. He even remembered my teachings of 'harm no living thing'. Daniel and his girlfriend Courtney were both in the vegang and were happily working in rescue. We chatted about our days at nursery school and I soon remembered not only him being a very kind child, but his lovely mum Carol, dad, and sister and their family of cats and small fluffies. It's one of life's proud moments when you realise that no act of kindness is ever wasted. A pleasure to meet such an outstanding young couple who had made incredibly kind life choices at such a young age.

I'm proud to say that I see young people doing wonderful things every day for animals at The Retreat. For example, Kitty Maxwell who at the age of just eight started fundraising for The Retreat by doing sponsored walks, raising hundreds of pounds. My niece Darcy at eight years old joined the vegang and arranged table sales in support of the centre. Two of my great-nephews Charlie and Alfie both volunteer at The Retreat and are already vegan. My other great nieces and nephews JJ, Lillie, Demi, Ellie, Elsa and Macy already show a deep love and bond for animals and have always helped at The Retreat – an exceptional living example of how we can live without harming or taking anything from animals.

CHAPTER FIFTEEN

ONE BAD APPLE

Before you embark on a journey to build a pioneering project like The Retreat or even use a spare bedroom to help animals, you may envisage many obstacles and problems. The obvious would be not enough funds and where to find more avenues of funding, followed by a lack of dedicated helpers at the start to carry out the husbandry or rescue work, not to mention the set-up costs, rent and finances to purchase a base, and lack of physical space to accommodate your project. In reality, these issues will never work against you and logical problem-solving solutions will see you through all of these.

The real obstacles are ones you would never have seen coming in a million years. Being so involved with a project you care deeply about will always keep you busy and focused so you may not be aware of the real obstacles and problems lurking around you. From my experiences and those of the rescue centres I work with and love, these obstacles or monsters don't come straight out of horror movies. These are monsters you know well, who manoeuvre themselves alongside you. They are the ones who worm themselves in, showing false vulnerabilities so just like with the animals you reach out to help with their healing. You provide them with love, care and support but it's never enough.

You must look deep into the offers of help from people, even ones professing to be friends. For those of you reading this with a good gut feeling should not sit back on your laurels; these narcissists are very good at getting what they want, and you too may fall victim one day. If we had the time to delve deep into their backgrounds, we would find a path of destruction, a line of ruined lives that they cruelly crushed. Their only goal is their own gain and at whatever cost to those around them. They steal, lie, break up friends and families and worst of all have not a single care for helping animals. My warning is harsh for it's hard to escape their catatonic spell.

The good people of this world will find it hard to believe that such darkness fills some people but it does and I've learnt the hard way too – there are many of these people out there and they are our biggest obstacle. Rescue centres are especially vulnerable to these dysfunctional cruel types. They see a wealth of kindness and confuse it for weakness, yet we wouldn't be here today if we were the weak one. Our centres welcome those in who fool us with false claims of caring for animals when in fact they are monsters to animals too and have no regard for you or your project. But there is hope, just like at the end of the movie *The Wizard of Oz* when Dorothy throws water over the wicked witch and it destroys her. We have that power too. Just by shutting them out dismissing them from our lives you are in fact throwing the water over the witch. They need the drama to survive and will never lead a normal loving life. Our power is also to kill them with success and bury them with a smile. Move on and never say their name again.

One helper who told such elaborate lies when he arrived

that you could only believe them. He told us he had fought behind enemy lines in Afghanistan in an epic battle – something straight out of *Saving Private Ryan*, he claimed his helicopter had been shot down, that they had crash-landed, and he had miraculously survived. The walking wounded were picked up and rescued in a heroic fantasy, but his injuries could not be repaired so he was discharged on medical grounds. His sketchy past should have raised alarm bells, but the occasional theatrical head shake and tales of PTSD kept you open-minded to his struggle. In the end he could not keep up with his countless own charades and one by one they fell in front of him.

The fantasist was exposed and rather than facing the music in fear of becoming the laughing stock, he did a moonlight flit in our horse lorry. He filled up the lorry with our sit-on-mower, power tools and one of our dogs Luna and disappeared into the night. It took us a while but thankfully we found Luna after he no longer had any use for her. Stories emerged of him tipping baskets of terrified rats to his terrier dog and selling animals he obtained from rescues to top up his benefits before he came to The Retreat. These sad claims turn out to be true and came out during our investigations to find Luna.

We have taken the most desperate of people into our home and provided for them when they have stolen everything they can get their hands on. One woman, the dictionary definition of narcissist, came into our home after finding out she was pregnant by a convicted sex pest and could no longer keep a roof over the family's head. We offered her shelter and a place to heal. We cared for her children whilst she still had more, knowing she could not care for those she already had. Attempts to kill her own unborn child were not uncommon and I desperately offered to adopt the child to save its life. Even after birth the cruelty to her children continued whilst her eldest stole everything she could from the very home provided for her when she had nothing. Not surprising, that child had a cocaine addiction. With the mother drunk and unable to get out of bed she spent her life dreaming up reasons why she couldn't pull herself together. She would even tell people she was an ethical vegan when she ate in McDonald's three times a week and enjoyed a fish meal on occasions. Despite swearing she loved the animals, her job at The Retreat was sadly neglected, yet nothing could convince her that she was wrong.

Her hatred for anyone doing a good job within rescue was the very thing that she should have learnt from, but she couldn't accept fault. The green-eyed monster set her destruct button every time. The lack of love she showed her own children was reflected in the fact she verbally attacked her husband so badly that he died in front of her child many years before. She took over our lives and we struggled to find a way to break free from her intimidating and manipulating behaviour. We eventually found the courage to have her removed from our home and the centre, realising she was not ill but toxic.

Humans – and not the ones you think you will have trouble with – will be your biggest challenge in any project like The Retreat. I can only stress the importance of getting references and looking deep into the person offering help. Look at who surrounds them and if they have no long-term friends or a clear history don't touch them with a barge pole. Evil hides itself well behind a mask of vulnerabilities.

Remember the story of Snow White. Her wicked stepmother was the original narcissist; her anger and hate ran deep whilst Snow White, with her love for the natural world, lived her successful idyllic life away from her. The stepmother disguised her evil with the vulnerabilities of an old beggar woman and with the one bite of the apple she had you. Sadly, the illness of the wicked stepmother will never heal, nor will those who prey on the goodness of the world we live in. 'Better an empty room than a bad lodger' is a mantra I now live by. Evil is your only obstacle on this path, and it walks on two legs…

Chapter Sixteen

BE KIND, IT'S EASY

A beautiful tale of combining helping animals and people occurred one late afternoon on a rescue call. A contact in a cat rescue group had alerted me to a property in South East London where the council was going to kill a flock of pigeons living in a dilapidated house. It was only around the corner for me, so I went to save the day.

I turned up with nets, food and boxes to save the birds from the gun. The old Victorian house had many of its front windows boarded up and the overgrown garden was full of rubbish. I pushed open the side gate whilst waiting for the council contact to arrive. I climbed over years of rubbish and fought my way through the accidental wildlife refuge. The poor old house had seen better times and really was unloved. This was not a case of a lick of paint but a full renovation before the house collapsed. I feared it was structurally unsafe, but the birds needed my help.

I let myself into what was once a kitchen and avoiding the remnants of years of never throwing anything out I made my way through the hall over a horrendous collection of anything and everything covered in pigeon mess. I climbed the once grand staircase, over piles of newspaper and buckets of dirty water from catching the rain. With ceilings missing to the first floor I could then see up through the next floor and into the loft. With a broken loft window, the pigeons had happily set up hotel in the dry areas of the roof.

I was just going to collect my rescue equipment and maybe bump into the council worker when what I thought was a ghostly image appeared from one of the rooms. It was an older lady smartly dressed, with the thickest of long grey hair and beautiful skin.

'Hello,' she said in the politest of voices. 'Can I help you?'

My heart stopped; this was like a scene from *Most Haunted*. Was she real, or was it my lack of sleep? Was she a good ghost or a bad ghost? My knees were shaking like Shaggy from *Scooby Doo*. We carried on staring at each other and finally she held out her delicate hand.

'I'm Shirley,' she said with a cheeky grin, clearly aware she'd scared the life out of me. 'Are you Billy from the cat group?'

This softly spoken woman actually lived in this damp, dark and forgotten home. Her husband Dennis had died years ago, and since then she had struggled with the upkeep of the house. Being a real animal lover she lived in harmony with over thirty pigeons in her loft. I explained I had to take the birds before the council killed them, and she wholeheartedly agreed.

I climbed into the loft and fed the birds. I waited for all to settle down and start to eat the corn. I slowly closed the broken loft window on the pigeons. No one could escape. With Shirley and now the council worker calling up into the loft to see if I'd got one yet, I caught the precious birds one by one, thinking about how they had flown against all the perils to deliver crucial messages during the war. Pigeons were also used to spot stranded seaman in the seas from aircraft during wartime conflict. Pigeons were the forgotten heroes of the free world and deserved our respect. If I were asked to help pigeons I always would, they deserved my help. Pigeons also feature in the English sculptor David Backhouse 2004 The Animals in War Memorial in Hyde Park – a fitting tribute to such courageous creatures who had no choice over their role.

On catching the last bird and picking up the featherless young I was faced with an unusual dilemma: what to do with the ghostly but cute old lady. She couldn't remain living here, the winter would kill her. It didn't take much for me to decide that if I wasn't going to leave a pigeon behind, I certainly wasn't leaving Mrs Meaker from *Rentaghost*.

'Come on,' I said, 'get your stuff, you're coming home with me.' She didn't argue and the council worker seemed happy to see the back of her. Shirley gathered a few shopping bags of her many things and we set off. She was ready for some help and I was certainly her knight in shining armour. How would I explain this rescue to Neil?

Neil was not surprised to find I had moved her in whilst he was at work. Shirley settled well into her new environment and adored the many animals she found sleeping on her bed. She never really questioned why she was now living with us but showed such gratitude. She came out on rescues with me any time, night or day and being gregarious enjoyed nothing better than a good get-together. Shirley's sense of justice ran deep inside her and on one occasion I asked where she had been all day and to my amazement she said, 'I took the train uptown to talk to the mayor of London.' To my surprise two weeks later a letter from the mayor of London's office arrived thanking her for coming in and voicing her concerns? *The dark horse*, I thought. Shirley was a great house guest and kept us on our toes with stories of her determination and courage throughout her life. For the best part of a year Shirley stayed with us, until we could eventually relocate her to a best friend in her local area. Her friend, also an animal lover, had cats and dogs so fitted in well. I really missed Mrs Meaker!

Animals will never disappoint you – in fact they will only ever enhance your life. Each one is an individual work of living art, and a miracle of life. In rescue we meet many people who overlook the wonders of animals. We refer to these people as 'SAD' which stands for Serial Animal Dumper. These people continually give up on their animals and move onto the next, never knowing the joy of helping those who need them. They are many and come from all different backgrounds. A SAD is a person who cannot see the beauty in the individual creature and is all about the next fix of a cute new animal. Usually they are not cruel people but don't realise they are the opposite to what they see themselves as; they are disconnected to the creatures sitting lovingly in front of them. Animals will always amaze you and counteract the negativity. Animals will answer all your questions and if you listen, they will talk not with words but actions because after all action speaks louder than words.

Thomas, a huge dairy bullock that shared our life for ten years, swept away the mound of earth on Merlin, his newly buried friend's grave, bellowing for help to resurrect his life partner in an unprecedented act of love. Jill the cow, on meeting three newly rescued day-old calves, hid behind Parsnip the sheep for support. Shaking like a feather, she didn't understand she was once a calf because her family was a sheep called Parsnip. Anton, the sheep who identifies as a horse, will not share field or barn with other sheep. He finds it upsetting if ever separated from his horse family where he knows he belongs. Mr Darcy and Mr Ellie, two eight-year-old brother ducks, never left each other's side from dusk 'til dawn. They grazed and swam together every day until Mr Darcy's death.

Brotherly love and the power of unity taught us about the emotional lives of sibling animals.

Paulo, a disabled pigeon, lived in the house for six years just like a dog. Eventually Paulo fell in love with a new intake and each day could be found outside the hospital cage of his new partner Choco. Toffee the pig is a very good mother. She was due to have her babies any day when she broke her leg. Blank-faced vets could not fix her leg, because she was a pig and not a dog. Then entered the world-renowned Noel Fitzpatrick of *The Supervet* fame, who offered help to fix her leg and three days later she gave birth to eleven healthy babies. Even though her leg was now in external fixators she only worried about her new-borns and caring for them.

Basil the goose loved his human companions and had lived with Clare and Arthur for over two decades. Sadly, old age and health problems meant that Clare and Arthur had to say goodbye to Basil. Basil needed to find a new safe place to live and The Retreat agreed to take him. On arrival he chose his favourite team members – Rose and Ken – and loved them unconditionally. He would even push open doors to share tea breaks with Rose. He knew the sound of Ken's engine and would be in the car park to greet him.

Bramble Bill was one magnificent turkey. He had his fan club and even a human wife. Mrs Bramble Bill was Constance, who lived in London but from their first meeting fell in love. There's no doubt that absence made the heart grow fonder and Bramble made more of a fuss when seeing his wife after prolonged periods. He never failed to spot her through the crowds of adoring fans. Alex the cockerel was the star of the cafe. He would enjoy his regular chips and salad with his best friends. Sally and Mark were definitely his favourite and in spotting them would hang around until Sally proudly picked him up and sat him on her lap.

A wonderful support system from three independent vets enable us to provide the best services for our rescues. We are proud to work with such independent enterprises. The vets and support staff of Badgers Oak Vets, with George at the helm, serve our farm animal residents well. George is celebrated with having an eye for early diagnosis and we are always grateful for his input. Vicki and Katie from Heronden vets look after the smaller animals of The Retreat. Vicki has very kindly accompanied me on call-outs to sick and abandoned foals in our local area, giving me valuable advice and action to take. RW Equine vets Northiam, with Ruben at the helm followed by Harriet and a team of devoted staff, support our equine residents. Ruben is famous for loading any naughty horse and solving complex cases and not charging us the earth.

In everyone's journey, wherever you are and whatever you're doing, there's room to help an animal. There's still enough time to sit at home with a drink, read your favourite book, eat pizza and travel. Even dare to have a life but just remember one rule: 'Nurture them all pretty or plain, young or old, abled or disabled for you would expect the same'. Make room in your life for feeding the wildlife in the park or local open space if you have no garden. Help out at a rescue centre which will cost you nothing, even if it's dropping off newspaper you have collected like dear friends of The Retreat John, Wendy and Flora the dachshund do. Pop along with a few tins of pet food like Mary and her greyhound do, or give up your Christmas Day just like Yvonne the Elf. Be part of the bigger picture and be part of the change.

My journey for animals has been amazing and will continue and I know with all you by my side it will be just as colourful – and hopefully enough for another book. I'm just one ordinary man trying to do an extraordinary thing with the support of some great people. Be kind, it's easy.

THE END

ACKNOWLEDGEMENTS

All those darling animals who changed my destiny for the better and the residents of The Retreat. My husband Neil, Mum, Dad and my sister Lil. Aunty Betty and Peter. My managers, Rose and Scott, and The Retreat teams.

The Farm team: Sorrell, Fleur, Sarah N, Sam L, Jake, Jasmin, Morag, Louis S, Helen, Ken, Connor, Ollie, Sam J, Charlotte, Emily, Louise, Dave and Emma, Louis F, Hannah and Diego, Miracle.

The Horse team: Gina, Angie, Marion, Fran, Sarah, Kate, Pash, Sam H, Charlie, Alfie, Leeanna, Amelia, Sandra, Georgia, Lori, Sue, Thirza.

The Cat team: Sophie, Heidi, Jan, Nicki and Zoe.

Treatment Zone: Sarah P.

Shop: Val.

Café: Jane, Chris, June, Amy and Adam.

Maintenance man Peter Reynolds, John the Digger.

The Flair Foundation Feeders: Carol and Jackie.

The Retreat's Trustees: Lil, Cara, Mandie, Alex and Kerrie.

Pat and Peter French, Richard Thoburn, June Maloney and Tony Whitehead, Eddy French, Dr Susan Bauer, Anthony Keen, Sue Woodhouse, Scarlet and Sebastian, Pam and Ian, Gabi and Hans Keller, Peter Eagle, Gloria and Jamie, Maureen Young, Sandy Ritson, Jane Chubb, Danuta Mayer, Andrea Charlwood, Regan and Jerry of Next Chapter, Annie and Roy at Animals in Need, Karen Shiver, PJ, Su and Ronnie, Brian Saville, Pantelis and Everlina, Jeneen Peter and

Morgan, Collette Marshal at the Kit Wilson Trust For Animal Welfare, Squirrel mummies Pam and Sally, Hilda and Laura at Foal Farm Animal Rescue, Friends of Feral Cat Group, Vicki Hammond, Jasmine Harman, Hayley at PetMeds, Kathy, Sonia, Phil and Jill, Mel Arnold, Angie Hamp and Mick, Katy and Kirsty, Saudi Alison and family, Alison Dave and Vicky Baker.

The Alpha Team: Sally, Mark, Kat, Scott and Harrison Giles.

Sally Queen of Raffles. Planet Earth Kitchen. The Vegan Babes. Debz. Catherine and Katie at The Green Kitchen Brighton. Rob, Anita and Naia at Vegan Edge. Lollipops, Jo and Dave at Woodlark Design. Teresa Wildflowers Favours. Books by Nora Rose. Chocolate Rox. Rob and Carman at Mad Ideas. Isabel and Cliff Martin. Ann-Marie from Sheds Of Love. Jo and Jason at Ethel Loves Me Rye. Joyce Walker. Donna Ross and Chloe Jennings for their incredible bravery.

My heroes of inspiration: Vicky Moore at FAACE, Wendy Valentine at Hillside Animal Sanctuary, Celia Hammond at The Celia Hammond Animal Trust, Jill Robinson at Animal Asia, Paula and Ernie Clark at Hopefield Animal Sanctuary.